Deconstructing WikiLeaks

Daniel Estulin

DECONSTRUCTING WIKILEAKS

Published by:
Trine Day LLC
PO Box 577
Walterville, OR 97489
1-800-556-2012
www.TrineDay.com
publisher@TrineDay.net

Library of Congress Control Number: 2012944882

Estulin, Daniel
Deconstructing WikiLeaks—1st ed.
p. cm.
Includes references and index.
Epud (ISBN-13) 978-1-937584-12-2
Mobi (ISBN-13) 978-1-937584-13-9
Print (ISBN-13) 978-1-937584-11-5
1. WikiLeaks (Organization). 2. Assange, Julian. 3. Leaks (Disclosure
of information) -- Political aspects -- United States. 4. Official secrets
-- United States. 5. Afghan War, 2001-. 6. United States -- Foreign rela-
tions -- 21st century. I. Estulin, Daniel. II. Title

FIRST EDITION
10 9 8 7 6 5 4 3 2 1

Printed in the USA
Distribution to the Trade by:
Independent Publishers Group (IPG)
814 North Franklin Street
Chicago, Illinois 60610
312.337.0747
www.ipgbook.com

Publisher's Foreword

We have, in the process, become the publisher of last resort.
—Julian Assange, Oslo Freedom Forum 2010

Freedom of the press is guaranteed only to those who own one.
A. J. Liebling, *The New Yorker* 1960

Well, don't we live in a wild world! How is one to know whom to believe. Some say this, some say that. All we know much of the time is simply what a journalist has written. We weren't there, nor do we have the time to check it out. We rely on our journalists to tell us what's going on. It's worrisome that most of them now work for just six megacorporations.

So, like most of the world's citizens, I was happy to hear about WikiLeaks and its mission: "to bring important news and information to the public...."

By late summer of 2012, Assange had taken asylum in the Ecuadoran Embassy in London, and WikiLeaks announced that "its cash reserves have sunken from around $983,600 in December 2010 to less than $120,000 at the end of June [2012]." And: "In order to effectively continue its mission, WikiLeaks must raise a minimum of EUR 1 million immediately."

Being a publisher myself, I realize it is quite easy to spend money; publishing isn't cheap. But I do have to ask, where does WikiLeaks' money go? TrineDay's biggest expenses are printing books, royalties to authors and promotion. WikiLeaks doesn't produce hard copy books, doesn't pay royalties, nor does it pay for promotion ... WikiLeaks gets worldwide publicity from the same six megacorporations.

That was always my biggest concern about WikiLeaks, how did they get the support of such prestigious news organizations (owned by the six megacorporations)? TrineDay is and has been a "publisher of last resort," and we get absolutely no support from news organizations. Matter-of-fact, we get roadblocks thrown in our way and are generally completely ignored. We have hired big guns in the PR world only to receive high-class written rejections instead of simply being brushed aside. We have sent books to all major news organizations, and politicos we could think of. We have called press conferences in major cities in America, generally filling the room – common people thirsting for good information – but never more than one media person. (One time it was a guy who had a two-hour hunting and fishing radio show on Saturday. God bless him, he did a wonderful interview with our suppressed author.)

So when I see Assange receiving *The Economist's* New Media Award and being made person of the year by *Time*, I have to wonder what's going on, especially when people from those same organizations are attendees at the annual Bilderberg Group conference ... but never report on it.

Which brings us to Daniel Estulin's new book, *WikiLeaks Deconstructed*. Estulin's exposé on the Bilderberg Group put the nail in the coffin of the canard that the Bilderberg group didn't really exist and the whole secret conclave was just the product of a conspiracy theorist's imagination. *WikiLeaks Deconstructed* takes us deep into the wilderness of smoke and mirrors, examining the truth behind WikiLeaks' claims, who Julian Assange is and exactly who has benefited from the releases of "secret" information.

Author Estulin brings together many different voices examining WikiLeaks' record and their journey from 2006 up to the present: Challenging the widespread media view and conventional wisdom on what WikiLeaks is and whom it serves.

Estulin's *WikiLeaks Deconstructed* takes us on a journey, many of us would rather not take. For I am sure all of us would like that WikiLeaks to be the real deal, but as author George R.R. Martin said, "Heroes are created by popular demand, sometimes out of the scantiest materials, or none at all."

Onwards to the utmost of futures!

Peace,
Kris Millegan
Publisher
TrineDay
August 3, 2012

Contents

Prologue

This is a book about WikiLeaks. Nothing strange in that, given that over the next few months we will be seeing hundreds if not thousands of books written by WikiLeaks insiders, outsiders, oversiders, media pundits, political activists from both the left and the right, politicians, social and political commentators and Michael Moore.

Along with hundreds of thousands of articles on Assange and his goofy entourage, we will have an inside story from Assange's personal butler, his hairdresser, his next door neighbor, the people who worked, lived, smoked, drank and had sex with Assange. These stories will be goosed with journalistic and lawyerly flim-flam to awaken readers and juries dozing with disinterest. We will be inundated with "real life" stories of "real people" who will tell us things "how they are," salted with dramatic examples of what will be "revealed for the first time."

Most people believe WikiLeaks to be a paragon of virtue and true blue, grass roots journalism. "With ambassadors resigning, diplomats being exposed as liars, political rift developing between Western imperial allies, not to mention careers and reputations ruined,"[1] WikiLeaks is supposedly creating the conditions to effectively undermine imperialism. Everyone from Fidel Castro to Putin, from Hugo Chavez to Evo Morales, from Mahmud Ahmedinejad to democratically elected leaders and dictators across the globe are using WikiLeaks to push their own interpretation of the events, consulting the WikiLeaks cables as if it were the Holy Scrip-

1

tures. If WikiLeaks is God and is our ally, who will dare to stand against us and against the word of God?

And, so it goes.

What none of these books will admit is that the "original WikiLeaks initiative is dead, replaced by a bloated publicity apparatus."[2] WikiLeaks was once an alternative to conventional sources of information ... or so we initially thought.

None of these books will tell you that WikiLeaks is a conspiracy reaching deep into the inner sanctums of the National Security Agency and the Central Intelligence Agency. WikiLeaks is an officially sanctioned covert operation that takes us into a "netherworld of intrigue, compartmentalization, secret operations and contrived situations," as my American publisher Kris Millegan has written in the Publisher's Forward to *Me & Lee:*

> Where one can be for or against something or a someone, depending on whichever guise is called up by a taskmaster giving the high sign through the shadows of plausible deniability: a wilderness of chicanery, deceit and double/triple crosses.
>
> Spin Control, Perception Management, Reality Engineering, Operation Mockingbird, whatever you wish to call it: the strategic psychological operations designed to manipulate our media and our own perceptions of reality and cover up the mega misdeeds of flagrant corruption.
>
> Agnotology is the scientific study of culturally induced ignorance: such as when intelligence agencies or other shadow players use their behind-the-scenes capabilities of media spin to conceal scurrilous activities and agendas.[3]

The cost of this mercenary connivance, Kris Millegan said, "is our heritage, our liberty, our freedom, our country and ... our future. This book gives you the opportunity to understand the depth of the lies and the deception by the people with long-ranged secret agendas."

This fascinating conspiracy puzzle will take us from a wandering theatre company in Australia to macabre mind control experiments, cults, secret societies, Nazi rituals, billionaires, think-tanks and foundations with far-reaching agendas, and implicates the White House, the Pentagon and the CIA. And in the middle of it all is a mysteriously strange, robotic character named, Julian Assange.

As Author Peter Levenda wrote about his own book, *Sinister Forces*, "Some of you will throw this book across the room, then get around to picking it up and reading a little further before you throw it down again in a fury at the uneasy possibility that the story you have been told by the mainstream, corporate press, may be an outright lie at best or a planned and well orchestrated conspiracy at worst."

But, as much as you would wish to deny its existence, logic is a finicky thing. And so is the truth.

Truth always lies in the higher order of processes. True sovereignty lies not in popular opinion, but in the creative powers of the individual human mind. And as I stated during my press conference on the Bilderberg group at the European Parliament in Brussels on June 1, 2010, "Until we can bring mankind into the Age of Reason, our understanding of reality will be shaped in actuality, not by the wills of masses of humanity, but by the mere handfuls who, for purposes of good or evil, steer the fate of mankind generally as herds of cows are steered to and from the pasture—and, occasionally, also to the slaughter-house."

Daniel Estulin
February 23, 2011
Madrid, Spain

(ENDNOTES)

1   Andrew Gavin Marshall, "WikiLeaks and the Worldwide Information War," globalresearch.ca, December 6, 2010.

2   John Young, "WikiLeaks Rest in Peace," cryptome.org, December 30, 2010.

3   Kris Millegan, *Me & Lee*, publisher's forward, TrineDay, 2010.

4   Peter Levenda, *Sinister Forces*, TrineDay, 2006.

5 Daniel Estulin, *Shadow Masters: An International Network of Governments and Secret-Service Agencies Working Together with Drugs Dealers and Terrorists for Mutual Benefit and Profit*, TrineDay, 2010.

Chapter 1

Through The Looking Glass

U p until four years ago, nobody had ever heard of WikiLeaks, but the fact is, it is becoming massively important. There are currently over 74,000,000 references to WikiLeaks on Google. It has been said that in just three years, WikiLeaks has published more scoops than the Washington Post has in thirty. The operating manual from the Guantanamo prison camp was leaked by the group, and most recently, a CIA report on how to manipulate public opinion in France and Germany with the goal of keeping their troops in Afghanistan.

During his live television show, Brian Lehrer asked Salon's columnist Glen Greenwald and Cryptome's John Young: "So, what does it mean when anyone can post secret information on line? Is it a wonderful new era of openness and citizen journalism or is it an irresponsible age in which governments, corporations and individuals become embarrassed, ineffective and even in danger."[1] No matter how one decides to look at it, WikiLeaks represents a change to the status quo, an international and non-corporate interference into the business of information; a brown paper envelope of the digital age, striking fear into the heart of everyone with something to hide.

Or so it seems.

But there is more to WikiLeaks than meets the eye.

"There is an old English expression ... that a man is known by the company he keeps. What I find significant however, is the company WikiLeaks keeps, especially the funny organizations and foundations they call friends."[2]

WikiLeaks had also entered into negotiations with several corporate foundations with a view to securing funding.[3]

As Adam K. East reports in *Executive Intelligence Review*, "A closer look at the activities of these private agencies reveals that there was much more at stake.... The source of policy for most of these groups was Anglo-American intelligence"[4] and their One World Company planners. "As such, these groups lobbied the U.S. Congress, set up conferences, launched propaganda campaigns, and, in some cases, even provided military training for various mujahideen groups,"[5] while simultaneously supporting oppressive dictatorships around the world.

For example, part of the "process of cooptation is implemented and financed by US based foundations including the National Endowment for Democracy (NED) and Freedom House (FH)."[6]

Freedom House is a Washington based organization founded in 1941 by Leo Cherne to promote American entry into World War II. "During the Cold War, [it was used] as a vehicle for CIA-directed anti-communist propaganda. Its recent activities have been a central role as NGO in Washington-directed destabilization [efforts] in Tibet, Myanmar, Ukraine, Georgia, Serbia and other countries apparently not pursuing policies satisfactory to certain powerful people in the USA."[7]

> Amongst its marquis projects, it launched the American Committee for Peace in Chechnya (ACPC). Jeffrey Steinberg, writing for the EIR reports that, "The goal of the group was unabashed: to interfere into the internal affairs of Russia under the doublespeak slogan that the 'Russo-Chechen war' must be settled 'peacefully.'"[8]

Freedom House is another funny organization, that under the cover of benevolent, peace-loving mover of democratic reform "has worked closely with George Soros' Open Society Institutes ... in promoting such projects as the 2005 Tulip Revolution in Kyrgyzstan that brought the Washington-friendly dictator and drug boss, Kurmanbek Bakiyev to power."[9]

Steinberg made it quite clear when he stated in his September 17, 2004 *Executive Intelligence Review* article, "A review of the group's leading members reveals that this is anything but a bunch of peaceniks. The founding chairs of the group [ACPC] were Brzezinski, former Reagan Secretary of State Alexander "I'm in Charge Here" Haig, and former Congressman Stephen Solarz (D-N.Y.). Members include: Elliott Abrams, Kenneth Adelman, Richard Allen, Richard Burt, Eliot Cohen, Midge Decter, Thomas Donohue, Charles Fairbanks, Frank Gaffney, Irving Louis Horowitz, Bruce Jackson, Robert Kagan, Max Kampelman, William Kristol, Michael Ledeen, Seymour Martin Lipset, Robert McFarlane, Joshua Muravchik, Richard Perle, Richard Pipes, Norman Podhoretz, Arch Puddington, Gary Schmitt, Helmut Sonnenfeldt, Caspar Weinberger, and James Woolsey. ACPC operates out of Freedom House and the Jamestown Foundation, a Cold War-era Washington think-tank which includes Brzezinski and Woolsey on its board, and which boasts a mission of conducting 'democracy'-promoting operations inside 'totalitarian' states."[10]

Freedom House has "connections and/or are affiliated to a number of establishment organizations, major corporate foundations and charities"[11] has been confirmed from WikiLeaks-published email exchanges at the outset of the project on January 4, 2007. This included an invitation to Freedom House (FH) to participate in the WikiLeaks advisory board:

> We are looking for one or two initial advisory board member from FH who may advise on the following:
> 1. The needs of FH as consumer of leaks exposing business and political corruption.
> 2. The needs for sources of leaks as experienced by FH.
> 3. FH recommendations for other advisory board members.

4. General advice on funding, coalition [sic] building and decentralised operations and political framing.[12]

Furthermore, "both FH and the NED have links to the US Congress, the Council on Foreign Relations (CFR), and the US business establishment. Both the NED and FH are known to have ties to the CIA."[13]

"National Endowment for Democracy, the congressionally created funding conduit for Project Democracy"[14] is a top-secret project with a clear cut objective: undermine any and all governments around the world whose interests do not coincide with the publicly stated long range interests of the United States government. In his fabulous piece on the protest movement in Egypt, Michel Chossudovski writes that "The NED is actively involved in Tunisia, Egypt and Algeria. Freedom House supports several civil society organizations in Egypt,"[15] funded through the U.S. State Department.

The history of National Endowment for Democracy reads like a John Le Carré novel, full of sinister characters, behind-the-scenes covert agendas and special interests that when taken together, have very little to do with promoting democracy throughout the planet. "The NED was established by the Reagan administration after the CIA's role in covertly funding efforts to overthrow foreign governments was brought to light, leading to the discrediting of the parties, movements, journals, books, newspapers and individuals that received CIA funding…. As a bipartisan endowment, with participation from the two major parties, as well as the AFL-CIO and US Chamber of Commerce, the NED took over the financing of foreign overthrow movements, but overtly and under the rubric of 'democracy promotion.'"[16]

Among the plethora of private "aid" agencies and think-tanks with direct links to Freedom House, providing active support and which stand out head and shoulders above the rest is the little known but extremely powerful and well-connected group – Afghan Aid. What does an organization involved with Afghanistan have to do with Egypt? Nothing, except that it forms a part of the interlocked apparatus of financial and political interests linked to Freedom House. With the ostensible aim of helping the political opposition in Egypt, these agencies have provided massive "overt and covert funding for black operations by various U.S. governmental agencies"[17] not only in Egypt, but also in Russia, Africa, South America and the Middle East. For example, Afghan Aid, was the primary organization to massively support Afghan 'mujahideen' (holy warriors), as they came to be known at the time of Soviet invasion.

> The main sponsor and funder of the group was Viscount Cranbourne, Lord Privy Seal (chief of the Queen's Privy Council), and Leader of the House of Lords.
>
> Viscount Cranbourne is a member of the Cecil family, one of the oldest and most powerful oligarchical families in Britain, whose ancestor, Lord Burghley, was the Lord Privy Seal and Lord Treasurer of Queen Elizabeth I. Viscount Cranbourne is the son and heir to the current Sixth Marquis of Salisbury. His grandfather, the Fifth Marquis, had been a British colonial secretary in World War II, and a post-war foreign minister, as well as having been Lord Privy Seal and Leader of the House of Lords. His great-great-grandfather, the famous Third Marquis of Salisbury, had been the British prime minister and foreign minister from 1878-87, and again 1900-02; he helped lay the basis for World War I.[18]

In other words, WikiLeaks is looking to plug into financial and intellectual support from some of the highest echelons of the ruling elite. Does that make sense? It does, if you come from a parallel universe of smoke and mirrors.

In a series of articles in the October 13, 1995 issue of the Executive Intelligence Review, titled "The Anglo-American support apparatus behind the Afghani mujahideen," another organization heavily involved in all kinds of subversive activities with links to the Freedom House was named the, Afghan Relief Committee(ARC). The ARC "was established in 1980 by Wall Street investment banker and spy John

Train, who handles the family fortunes of some of the oldest and most powerful U.S. establishment families, such as the Mellons.... CIA director William Casey was on the ARC's board of directors."[19] We will meet the Mellons, in all their splendor, later in our story.

The "stated purpose of the ARC was to raise 'seed money' for medical organizations treating casualties among the mujahideen."[20] However, its real operation was far more sinister. One of ARC's favorites was Gulbuddin Hekmatyar and his Hezb-i-Islami group as well as the Haqqani clan and the money raised was more often than not channelled into the warlords' pockets.

The names Gulbuddin Hekmatyar and the Haqqanis may not ring a bell with most readers, but they were and still remain the absolute favorites with the Central Intelligence Agency's long-range planners.

Gulbuddin Hekmatyar, one of the most sadistic warlords and drug traffickers, was on the CIA payroll and received more than $30 million during the war against the Red Army in the 1980s. Others who enjoyed the favors of the Agency were the Haqqani clan. Between 1980 and 1986, the CIA had given the Haqqanis $28 million, plus Stinger missiles and 4 tanks. The Haqqani immediately sold the tanks to the Soviets and when the war ended, the CIA bought back the Stingers for 10 times their value, paying nearly $400,000 for each. The Haqqanis, being honest and ethical, invested the money in al-Qaeda, making friends in the process with Osama bin Laden, several sheiks from Saudi Arabia and senior Pakistani intelligence.

Is this a case of the tail wagging the dog or a snake eating its own tail? Whichever it is, the interlocked nature of these organizations certainly gives one enough food for thought. "From its inception, the ARC worked closely with Freedom House, which had been chaired by Leo Cherne since the 1940s, and whose treasurer, Walter Schloss, was a long-time business associate of Train. Cherne was the vice-director of the President's Foreign Intelligence Advisory Board with offices at the White House. Cherne's Peshawar-based office was staffed mostly with Hekmatyar's gang."[21]

"The main known financial beneficiaries of ARC were Doctors Without Borders,"[22] founded by Bilderberg's own Bernard Couchner. "This organization, whose most prominent representative was Danielle Mitterrand, wife of President François Mitterrand of France, also received money from the National Endowment for Democracy."[23]

In a bitter irony and delicious example of political double-talk, the organizations supporting dictators, murderers, warlords and corrupt political agendas are the same groups WikiLeaks has been targeting for financial support. Why would that be, if we believe their anti-establishment propaganda? But are they really anti-establishment, and if not who do they work for and what long-sighted agenda do they represent? In this book, we will try to answer all of these questions.

MONEY FOR NOTHING

What remains WikiLeaks' best kept secret is the source of their funding. What is known is that, according to Assange, "the linchpin of WikiLeaks' financial network is Germany's Wau Holland Foundation.... Mr. Assange said WikiLeaks gets about half its money from modest donations processed by its website, and the other half from 'personal contacts,' including 'people with some millions who approach us....'"[24]

But, that's not their only source of funding. "According to email exchanges, acquiring covert funding from intelligence agencies was also contemplated."[25]

Back in early 2007, when very few people could have imagined that the WikiLeaks circus was coming to town, complete with albino jugglers, three-legged acrobats, belly dancers and a poetry-reciting cyclops, WikiLeaks acknowledged "that the project had been 'founded by Chinese dissidents, mathematicians and startup company technologists, from the US, Taiwan, Europe, Australia and South Africa.... [Its advisory board] includes representatives from expat Russian and Tibetan refugee communities, reporters, a former US intelligence analyst and cryptographers.'"[26]

Is it me, or is something obviously very fishy about this mix? So, who are some of the key players in the decision making process behind WikiLeaks?

One of the key players on the Board is Philip Adams, who "held key posts in Australian governmental media administration"[27] and contributed to the *Times*, the *Financial Times* in London and the *New York Times*. [Adams worked as a] columnist for the *Australian* since the 1960s. The *Australian* is owned by News Corporation, a property of Rupert Murdoch, member of the Council on Foreign Relations (CFR) and the Bilderberg Group. You could hardly call him anti-establishment. He is the representative of the International Committee of Index on Censorship[28] would it [surprise you to know] that WikiLeaks was awarded the 2008 Index on Censorship Freedom of Expression award.[29] How is that for a coincidence?

Another individual associated with WikiLeaks is Ben Laurie, a former security boss of Google, who denied knowledge of his involvement and further stated that "his only substantive interaction with the group was when Assange approached him to help design a system that would protect leakers' anonymity."[30]

Google has been associated with a proprietary investment company run by the CIA, In-Q-Tel, a public face of the National Security Agency, America's most powerful intelligence organization. On February 4, 2010, the Washington Post announced that "The world's largest Internet search company and the world's most powerful electronic surveillance organization are teaming up in the name of cybersecurity."[31] Cyber Security is a large hidden part of the WikiLeaks project, something they would rather you not know anything about. So, one of the people on the board of WikiLeaks comes from this environment.

Furthermore, Ben Laurie is a Director of Open Rights Group,[32] funded[33] by the Joseph Rowntree Reform Trust Ltd. and the Open Society Foundation. Open Society is funded by George Soros.

"*Time* magazine has characterized financier George Soros as a 'modern-day Robin Hood,' who robs from the rich to give to the poor countries of eastern Europe and Russia. It claimed that Soros makes huge financial gains by speculating against western central banks, in order to use his profits to help the emerging post-communist economies of eastern Europe and former Soviet Union, to assist them to create what he calls an 'Open Society.' The Time statement is entirely accurate in the first part, and entirely inaccurate in the second. He robs from rich western countries, and uses his profits to rob even more savagely from the East, under the cloak of 'philanthropy.' His goal is to loot wherever and however he can."[34]

What does not pass a smell test is the plethora of Chinese and Tibetan dissidents on WikiLeaks' Advisory Board. For example, one of the Board members is Tashi Namgyal Khamsitsang, a "Tibetan exile & activist"[35] is a former President of the Washington Tibet Association, and a member of the Tibetan Government-in-Exile. In July 2010, he was appointed by the Governor of Washington State to the State Commission on Asian Pacific American Affairs.

Another, "Wang Youcai, co-founded the Chinese Democracy Party and a leader of the Tiananmen Square protests. Imprisoned for conspiring to overthrow the Government of China... he was exiled in 2004 under international political pressure, especially from the United States. He is also a 'member of Chinese Constitutional Democratic Transition Research and a member of the Coordinative Service Platform of the China Democracy Party'"[36]

To most people old enough to have seen it on television, the Tiananmen Square student protests in Beijing in June

1989 are shrouded in the images of CNN and the lonely protester with a shopping bag, dressed in a white shirt and black trousers, blocking a column of tanks. But as F. William Engdahl writes, "What few know is that Tiananmen Square in June 1989 was an early attempt of the US intelligence to interfere in the internal affairs of the Peoples' Republic of China and to implement what later came to be called Color Revolutions. Similar Color Revolutions were later run by Washington in Serbia against Milosevic, in Ukraine with the so-called Orange Revolution, Georgia's Rose Revolution and other geopolitical destabilizations aimed at creating Washington-friendly regime changes."[37]

Strangely enough, or perhaps not, the advisory board members list no longer appears on WikiLeaks' website. "In the currently available description, the reference to the Chinese dissidents and the origins of the other members has been removed. WikiLeaks rather puts the emphasis on not being a covert operation"[38] If they are not a covert, intelligence-run operation, then why the cover-up and the secrecy?

Scott Creighton writes in globalresearch.ca December 11, 2010 edition: "You tack PR guys with News cork affiliations onto Chinese dissidents who have been probably funded by the CIA in times past... mesh that up with John Young's 2006 conclusions, and you come away with a different view of WikiLeaks altogether... especially when you look at the sum total of the work they have "leaked" over the years."[39]

Another key Chinese dissident involved in the WikiLeaks project is Xiao Qiang, "'founder and publisher of China Digital Times,' which is a grantee of the National Endowment for Democracy (NED)."[40] [He is also a commentator for] Radio Free Asia, "funded by the Broadcasting Board of Governors (BBG)"[41] which "encompasses all U.S. civilian international broadcasting, including the Voice of America (VOA), Radio Free Europe/Radio Liberty (RFE/RL), Radio Free Asia (RFA)."[42] The U.S. Congress, through the Central Intelligence Agency, provided initial funding for RFE and RL.

Qiang, too, is connected to Tiananmen, and received the MacArthur Fellowship from the John D. and Catherine T. MacArthur Foundation in 2001.[43]

The Catherine T. MacArthur Foundation is interlocked with Ford Foundation, Rockefeller Foundation and Andrew W. Mellon Foundation. These groups are the figureheads for a 37-year-old propaganda machine run through the Worldwatch Institute, which is bought and paid for by the environmentalist cartel interests whose objective is to reduce the world's population to a more manageable 2 billion people through aggressive de-population schemes. "Other Worldwatch funding agencies include the U.N. Environment Program, the U.N. Population Fund, the Rockefeller Brothers Fund,, the Winthrop Rockefeller Trust, the Lynn R. and Karl E. Pickett Fund, the Robert R. McCormick Charitable Trust, and the Pew Charitable Trusts"[44] Plus they receive funding from the Earth Institute and the Aspen Institute.

> The Earth Institute was created in 1995 in New York City ... to serve as a co-ordinating centre to push propaganda for global warming and offering the Malthusian doctrine of 'sustainable development' as an alleged solution.... The sustainable development mantra is that mankind, through industrialization ... is consuming 'finite resources' at an unsustainable rate. [Thus, the idea to de-industrialize the world in order to save the planet from itself.] The Earth's Institute director, Jeffrey Sachs, is notorious for enforcing 'shock therapy' on Russia, Poland, and several other Eastern European nations during the 1990s, after the fall of communism, which thereby produced precipitous drops in industrial production and mass unemployment....[45]

Jeffrey Sachs and company are well known to the readers of my book *Shadow Masters*. Sachs unleashed market reforms on Russia's proto-democracy, creating the collapse of the Russian economy. "This colonization, masked as reforms, destroyed the basic institutions of Russian society, the financial system of the state, its scientific and technological potential and transferred the rights to exploit the most valuable raw materials deposits to transnational corporations while establishing control over the Russian stock exchange."[46]

Who is behind the Earth Institute? Well, your usual characters. "The Rockefeller Brothers Fund has poured a large stream of money into the Earth Institute. The Institute counts among its Advisory Board members" Kenneth Arrow, a pioneer in "systems analysis"; and ... financier George Soros.[47] WikiLeaks has approached The Rockefeller Brothers fund for financial donations, but it is unknown whether anything came of it.

"The Rockefeller Foundation was created in 1913 by John D. Rockefeller out of the family's Standard Oil (today Exxon-Mobil and Chevron) fortune.... In the 1920s and the 1930s, the Rockefeller Foundation funded Germany's Kaiser Wilhelm Institute of Anthropology, Human Heredity and Eugenics, where Fritz Lenz and Eugen Fischer pioneered Nazi work on eugenics and 'racial hygiene.' ...The Standard Oil combine, along with the Rockefeller-owned Chase Manhattan Bank, were prime collaborators of Hitler and his Vichy puppet government in France. Together, the Rockefeller Foundation and the Rockefeller Brothers Fund have shovelled tens of millions of dollars into environmentalist projects operated by World Wildlife Fund and Greenpeace...."[48] But, it gets better!

Then, there is the Aspen Institute. "Aspen was founded by Robert Maynard Hutchins, the long-time chancellor of the University of Chicago, who was the leading American ally of the late Lord Bertrand Russell, the international socialist who advocated the elimination of science and the systematic elimination of the darker-skinned races.... To this day, Aspen is one of the leading Malthusian policy snake-pits in the world, peddling the idea of food as a weapon."[49] Why are all these environmentalist, anti-progress and leading Malthusian organizations congregating around WikiLeaks?

As Julie Lévesque writes, "Among the Chinese dissidents once listed on the board is Wang Dan. He was a leader of the Tiananmen Square democracy movement," which "earned him the top spot on China's list of '21 Most Wanted Beijing Student Leaders.'" He was imprisoned for his subversive activities and "exiled in 1998 under international political pressure to the United States."[50]

> He is chairman of the Chinese Constitutional Reform Association, and sits on the editorial board of Beijing Spring, a magazine funded by NED, the "chief democracy-promoting foundation" according to an article by Judith Miller in the *New York Times*. One of the founders of NED was quoted as saying "A lot of what we [NED] do today was done covertly 25 years ago by the CIA." (quoted in William Blum, *Rogue State: A Guide to the World's Only Superpower*, 2000, p. 180).[51]

So, the CIA=NED=Chinese Dissidents= Catherine T. Mac Arthur Foundation=Rockefeller Foundation=Malthusian de-population scheme=WikiLeaks.

Truth, when unravelled, is a million times stranger than fiction.

The question I have, again, is what are all these Tiananmen dissidents with links to CIA funding doing on the board of an alleged anti-establishment organization such as WikiLeaks? "The award of the Nobel Peace Prize to Liu Xiaobo was clearly no coincidence of events. Rather it must be understood in my view as a calculated part of a long-term strategy, not from a few members of the Norwegian Parliament, but from the leading elite circles of the world's hegemonic power, the United States, to break China's stride to become a sovereign and leading world economic factor. ...[This] is all part of an orchestrated deeper game, using 'human rights,' and a web of NGOs and organizations that Washington controls directly or indirectly, as a weapon of Washington geopolitics."[52]

As economist F. William Engdahl writes in October 2010 issue of oilgeopolitics.net, "Liu Xiaobo was President of the Independent Chinese PEN Center until 2007 and currently holds a seat on its board according to his official biography at the PEN International website. PEN is not just any random collection of writers. It is an integral part of the Anglo-American web of human rights and democracy advocacy NGOs and private organizations used to achieve defined geopolitical goals of its sponsors ... a network of private U.S. and European foundations. [Among them is Freedom House.] ...It aims to create something it calls a 'world culture.' That smells suspiciously like the Anglo-American theme of 'Global Governance' or David Rockefeller's 'New World Order.'[53]

Yet, it would be a fallacy to consider the New World Order merely a David Rockefeller project of domination. It has been an institutional consensus of the Anglo-American power establishment going back to the beginning of the 20th century.

DOWN THE RABBIT'S HOLE

Once removed from the individuals involved with the project, WikiLeaks' mandate takes an even grizzlier dip into the world of smoke and mirrors. According to an attribution on its own webpage: "[WikiLeaks will be] an uncensorable version of Wikipedia for untraceable mass document leaking and analysis. Our primary interests are oppressive regimes in Asia, the former Soviet bloc, Sub-Saharan Africa and the Middle East, but we also expect to be of assistance to those in the west who wish to reveal unethical behavior in their own governments and corporations."[54]

This mandate was confirmed by Julian Assange in a June 2010 interview in *The New Yorker*. "Assange also intimated that 'exposing secrets' 'could potentially bring down many administrations that rely on concealing reality—including the US administration.'"[55]

Would Hugo Chavez's Venezuela qualify as an oppressive regime? Of course it would, if you believe the mainstream U.S. press. Never mind that Venezuela has been a democracy and enjoyed free elections for the past half-century. You are a dictatorship if the United States government says you are. And with WikiLeaks' electronic trail of allegedly secret documents, that assessment has only been exacerbated.

Is independent Russia another oppressive regime whose secrets must be exposed for the good of One World Company limited? Subjugating Russia has been in the works since before the end of World War Two.

On the death of Roosevelt in April 1945, "President Harry Truman ordered General Eisenhower to prepare secret plans for a nuclear strike on some 20 cities of the Soviet Union.[56] The secret war plan was code-named TOTALITY. (JIC 329/1) Warplan TOTALITY was the first American plan to obliterate the Russian Heartland. It would by no means be the last.

> The Pentagon plan TOTALITY was never implemented. The detonation by the Soviet Union of its own atomic bomb in August 1949 caught the United States planners by total surprise. With the destruction of the Soviet Union in 1991, the US military industrial faction around the Pentagon and the US policy elites were ready to make a new try at achieving nuclear "first strike" superiority.[57]

Russia's deconstruction in the 1990s reminds us how easily you can defeat a powerful nuclear-armed enemy without firing a shot. It can be done through a combination of military and economic pressure with new tools such as NGOs, psychological warfare and fifth-column traitors, all run through allies within the very bosom of the Russian government. France in 1940 found itself embroiled in a similar situation, during the Nazi offensive, undermined by subversive synarchist elements within its own military.

In post-1991 Russia, the oligarchy became its fifth column. The New Russia created its own super-capitalist private funding forces in ways unmatched anywhere else in the world. With that money, these forces purchased services and loyalty at the highest levels of the Soviet bureaucracy.

The secret war against Putin's Russia took shape during the 2003 – 2004 period, that is, after Iraq and the Yukos affair – as the United States sights were once again turned to the defeat of Russia. American political leaders realized that geopolitical military conflict used against Yeltsin's Russia in the 1990s, based on agreements between the United States government, 'Yeltsin's Family', high level cronies in Yeltsin's entourage and the Russian army would be an utter failure with Putin at the helm. The essence of the agreements: Russia becomes America's junior partner with the country's raw materials included in the comprehensive settlement package in exchange for the 'stabilization' of the country. But Putin turned out to be a competent leader and a relentless negotiator, managing to play the Americans by refusing to support its attack on Iraq, while playing a clever game of pragmatism, flexibility and performance between Bush and the Franco-German duopoly of Chirac-Schroeder.

By December 2004, that plan had failed miserably, and both the U.S. and Britain realized that neither their reprehensible operations such as murdering of school-children in Beslan, nor their orange revolutions or guerrilla warfare in the North Caucasus were going to dislodge Putin from his presidential seat.

Something else was needed to subjugate Russia – an electronic trail of allegedly secret documents, asserting that an independent Russia is another oppressive regime whose secrets must be exposed for the good of 'world peace', 'democracy' and 'Open Society'.

In 2007, the unfinished business, as leading US policy circles saw it, was still to accomplish the utter and complete dismemberment of Russia as an independent nation state. "Nuclear missiles were but one piece of a vast arsenal of weapons and deceptions being deployed to encircle and ultimately destroy the one force left that could prevent a Total Global American Century, the realization of what the Pentagon termed Full Spectrum Dominance."[58]

· What is absolutely sure is that "from the outset, WikiLeaks' geopolitical focus on 'oppressive regimes' in Eurasia and the Middle East [an Orwellian double speak] was 'appealing' to America's elites, i.e. it seemingly matched stated US foreign policy objectives. Moreover, the composition of the WikiLeaks team (which included Chinese dissidents), not to mention the methodology of 'exposing secrets' of foreign governments, were in tune with the practices of US covert operations geared towards triggering 'regime change' and fostering 'color revolutions' in different parts of the World."[59]

Vladimir Putin

The latest attempt at discrediting Russia comes from the *Washington Post* article about the Russian WikiLeaks publication, Ru.Leaks. The object is to make Russia's government seem illegitimate by accusing them of excesses and corruption on a massive scale.

The pattern is quite easy to pick out. On January 17, 2011, Russian President Dmitry Medvedev called Iranian President Mahmoud Ahmadinejad and reaffirmed Russia's commitment to strengthen diplomatic ties with Iran.[60] Then on January 18, Medvedev recognized Palestine as an independent state during a visit to Jericho.

"So on Wednesday, the brand new WikiLeaks franchise in Russia published photos of what they claim are the billion dollar home Putin is supposedly building in Russia in an effort to embarrass the existing power structure in that country, namely Vladamir Putin, by calling them corrupt."[61] Is it me, or are we being played?

Putin may very well be corrupt, what politician isn't, but he's a far cry from the degeneracy that existed under alcoholic and usurper Boris Yeltsin, whose reign created the dreaded Russian oligarchs and opened the country up to international speculators who literally raped the nation and stole much of her wealth. Does anyone remember that?

The *Washington Post* notes that RuLeaks.net is a "version of WikiLeaks" but not actually run by Assange or anyone associated with WikiLeaks. Legally speaking, how is that possible?

According to *Raw Story*, an alleged anti-war, liberal publication, "the site opened in January 2011 and asked Russians to begin sending information on public corruption. In US diplomatic cables published by Assange's WikiLeaks, Russia was branded a 'mafia state,' and media estimates put annual profits by government officials from bribery alone at nearly $300 billion."[62]

Again, whose agenda is being served by these accusations?

MASS MEDIA CORP.

However, no (WikiLeaks) revolution can ever be successful without the key ingredient that has made all groundbreaking historical events possible – the role of the corporate media in manipulating public opinion. The greatest obstacle to discovery is not ignorance; it is the illusion of knowledge. And as Walter Lippmann said in his book titled *Public Opinion*, "News and the truth are not the same thing..."

William Norman Grigg, in an extensive article for *The New American* on the inner workings of the media cartel, astutely states that "Thomas Jefferson once famously remarked that it is better to have a newspaper without a government than a government without a newspaper. The free press, in whatever manifestation – plays an indispensable role in holding government accountable to the public. But the media "cannot perform this duty if it is itself part of the ruling Establishment – the self-appointed elitists like Rockefeller who busy themselves planning the future, supposedly on behalf of the 'whole of humanity."[63]

Nonsense, you say? The power elite would never conspire to consolidate economic and political power on a global scale." Many Europeans reacted in a similar way when they heard certain "alarmists" outside their mainstream media claim that elitists among them had created the Common Market for the purpose of gradually building it into a government of Europe. Now that the Common Market has become the EU through a series of steps, and the EU has begun sapping political and economic powers from once-sovereign European nations, a power grab once dismissed as preposterous is widely recognized as fact. But that power grab could not have succeeded without the complicity of the media moguls on both sides of the Atlantic, who portrayed earlier manifestations of the EU as a "free trade" agreement, thereby providing protective coloration for their counterparts in the political elite.[64]

The entire European edifice was and is based on lies. And as the European Union is crumbling into dust before our very eyes, these lies are being accentuated by the actions of the elite against the needs of its citizens. For example, "We were told, first of all, that the Lisbon Treaty is not the same as the original EU Constitutional Treaty. Come on, guys: everybody knows that the two texts are so similar that any claim to the contrary is either sophistry or an outright lie.

"It is true that some European leaders have joined in the sophistry to claim that the two documents are not the same. But the overwhelming majority concur with Valery Giscard d'Estaing's declaration that 'All the earlier proposals will be in the new text, but will be hidden and disguised in some way.' Next, it was argued by the Government that the Lisbon Treaty is no longer 'constitutional' and so does not require a referendum. This is a moot point, to say the least: the deal establishes a permanent EU presidency, an EU foreign minister, wide-ranging extensions of qualified majority voting, dramatic changes to the 'passerelle' or escalator system which enables the European Council unilaterally to extend its powers, and – perhaps above all – the Charter of Fundamental Rights, the precise legal significance of which Foreign Office lawyers admitted is unknowable in testimony to the Commons European Scrutiny Committee."[65]

ORIGINS OF THE MEDIA ELITE

"Control over the media has been a long-term objective of the globalist elite. In February, 1917, Congressman Oscar Callaway placed a statement in the Congressional Record describing the origins of what he called the 'newspaper combination.' According to that account, the J.P. Morgan Banking interests and their allies 'got together 12 men high up in the newspaper world and employed them to select the most influential newspapers in the United States and [the] sufficient number of them to control generally the policy of the daily press in the United States.'"

Beginning with a list of 179 papers, the 12 men pared down the list. Ultimately, the cabal "found it was only necessary to purchase control of 25 of the greatest papers. The 25 papers were agreed upon; emissaries were sent to purchase the policy, national and international, of these papers; an agreement was reached; the policy of the papers was bought, to be paid for by the month; an editor was furnished for each paper to properly supervise and edit information ... [on matters] considered vital to the interests of the purchasers."[66]

And as Marie Louise writes in "Operation Mockingbird: CIA Media Manipulation," "This concentration of ownership and power reduces the diversity of media voices, as news falls into the hands of large conglomerates with holdings in many industries that interferes in newsgathering, because of conflicts of interest."[67]

In that eye-opening piece for the *New American*, William Norman Grigg wrote, "In his 1966 work *Tragedy and Hope*, Quigley – after writing disdainfully of 'conspiracy theorists' – admitted the existence of a partially submerged elite that 'operates, to some extent, in the way the radical

Right believes the Communists act. In fact, this network, which we may identify as the Round Table Groups, has no aversion to co-operating with the Communists, or any other groups, and frequently does so. I know of the operations of this network because I have studied it for twenty years and was permitted for two years, in the early 1960s, to examine its papers and secret records.' The network's 'aim,' Quigley continued, is 'nothing less than to create a world system of financial control in private hands able to dominate the political system of each country and the economy of the world as a whole.'"[68] In other words, One World Company Ltd.

Grigg continues: "The 'Round Table Groups' stemmed from a secret society (Quigley's phrase) created by British magnate Cecil Rhodes to unite the world -- beginning with the English-speaking dominions – under 'enlightened' elitists like himself. World War I and the postwar proposal for a League of Nations resulted from the Round Table cabal's machinations. During the post-war Versailles 'Peace Conference,' noted Quigley, this covert network decided to establish 'in England and in each dominion, a front organization to the existing Round Table Group. This front organization, called the Royal Institute of International Affairs, had as its nucleus in each area the existing submerged Round Table Group. In New York it was known as the Council on Foreign Relations....'"[69]

John Galt in his *Beating the New World Order* explains: "On February 5, 1891, Cecil Rhodes established a secret society called the Circle of Initiates. Like most secret organizations, it had one individual or a very small group at the center and was surrounded by a series of concentric circles of outer members who were not privy to the secrets of the core but who supported its objectives.... There was an outer circle called the Association of Helpers, also called the Round Table Groups."[70]

In his documentary on the CFR, Servando Gonzalez explains that "The Round Table is later transformed by Colonel Edward Mandell House, [British economist] John Maynard Keynes, [economic historian] Arnold Toynbee, [Nazi supporter and former U.S. Secretary of State] John Foster Dulles and others into a publicly acknowledged formal council now known as Institute of International Affairs.... The conspirators decide to break down the Institute of International Affairs into an American branch, the Council on Foreign Relations, and a British branch, the Royal Institute for International Affairs."[71]

"Carroll Quigley, like David Rockefeller, specifically identified the *New York Times* and the *Washington Post* as key media organs of the power elite."[72] The *Washington Post*, founded by Eugene Meyer is the voice of official Washington, and has always stood for a weak presidency and ultimately for a strong Federal Reserve.

Historically, the *New York Times*, "with utterly unwarranted self-assurance, designates itself the arbiter of 'All the News that's Fit to Print.'"[73] "The *New York Times* has served the interests of the Rockefeller family in the context of a longstanding relationship. The current New York Times chairman Arthur Sulzberger Jr. is a member of the Council on Foreign Relations, son of Arthur Ochs Sulzberger and grandson of Arthur Hays Sulzberger who served as a Trustee for the Rockefeller Foundation. Ethan Bronner, deputy foreign editor of the *New York Times* as well as Thomas Friedman among others are also members of the Council on Foreign Relations (CFR).[74]

"America's corporate media and more specifically The New York Times are an integral part of the economic establishment, with links to Wall Street, the Washington think tanks and the Council on Foreign Relations (CFR)."[75] CFR is a US arm of the powerful and secretive Bilderberg Group. It is also, "the premier U.S. foreign policy think tank in the United States, and is one of the central institutions for socializing American elites from all major sectors of society (media, banking, academia, military, intelligence, diplomacy, corporations, NGOs, civil society, etc.), where they work together to construct a consensus on major issues related to American imperial interests around the world. As such, the CFR often sets the strategy for American policy, and wields enormous influence within policy circles, where key players often and almost always come from the rank and file of the CFR itself."[76] CFR's former President, Sir Winston Lord, made an interesting observation when he said that "The Trilateral Commission doesn't secretly run the world. The Council on Foreign Relations does that."[77]

The organization boasts a membership of about 4,000. "But its roster includes literally hundreds of powerful figures occupying key positions in the media – not merely writers, reporters, and news anchors who deliver the news, but also editors, publishers, and executives who define what news is and how it is covered. Just as significantly, the tiny CFR clique has for decades had a virtual stranglehold on the executive branch of the U.S. government, as well as much of academia."[78]

> In his October 30, 1993 'Ruling Class Journalists' essay, *Washington Post* ombudsman Richard Harwood candidly remarked about how the CFR dominates our news media. Harwood described the council as "the closest thing we have to a ruling Establishment in the United States.... [Its members are] the people who, for more than half a century, have managed our international affairs and our military-industrial complex.' After listing the executive branch positions then occupied by CFR members, Harwood continued: 'What is distinctively modern about the council these days is the considerable involvement of journalists and other media figures, who account for more than 10 percent of the membership."
>
> "The editorial page editor, deputy editorial page editor, executive editor, managing editor, foreign editor, national affairs editor, business and financial editor and various writers as well as Katharine Graham, the paper's principal owner, represent the *Washington Post* in the council's membership," observed Harwood. He went on to describe CFR representation among the owners, management, and edito-

rial personnel for the other media giants – the *New York Times, Wall Street Journal, Los Angeles Times*, NBC, CBS, ABC, and so on. These media heavyweights "do not merely analyze and interpret foreign policy for the United States; they help make it," he concluded…. Rather than offering an independent perspective on our rulers' actions, the Establishment media act as the ruling elite's voice – conditioning the public to accept, and even embrace, Insider designs that otherwise might not be politically attainable.[79]

PROPAGANDA CAMPAIGN

Even in the age of internet, blogospheres and other new generation contraptions of mass dissemination of information, the *Times* and the *Post*, (both Bilderberg and CFR companies) "set the tone for most news coverage, defining issues and setting the limits of 'respectable' opinion."[80]

Consider, for example, Sudan, to illustrate how the mainstream ruling class journalists "help make" foreign policy through a blatant propaganda campaign.

> Saturation reporting from a crisis region; emergency calls for help broadcast on the electronic media (such as the one recently on the BBC Radio 4 flagship Today programme); televised pictures of refugees; lurid stories of "mass rapes," which are surely designed to titillate as much to provoke outrage; reproachful evocations of the Rwandan genocide; demands that something must be done ("How can we stand idly by?," etc.); editorials [in the CFR run *New York Times*, the *Washington Post*, *Newsweek*, *Time* magazine and in CFR's own Foreign Policy magazine with long winded opinion pieces by Bilderberg-CFR member Zbiegniew Brzezinski] in the *Daily Telegraph* calling for a return to the days of Rudyard Kipling's benevolent imperialism; and, finally, the announcement that plans are indeed being drawn up for an intervention.[81]

The scenario for the intervention is easily copied and pasted from past historical events. As Keith Harmon Snow reports for *GlobalResearch* on February 7, 2007, "First: create instability and chaos that gives the appearance of Arabs fighting Africans (it's always those other people over there killing each other). Second: wage a media campaign that focuses a laser beam of public attention on the rising instability. Third: whip up public opinion and fury among a highly manipulated Western population who will, quite literally, believe anything. Fourth: make sure the devil—this time it's the Janjaweed—comes on horseback. This latter point underscores the tight, unwavering narrative of good versus evil. Fifth: demonize the "enemy" (read: dirty A-Rabs) and their partners (Chinese oil companies). Sixth: onward Christian soldiers and their "humanitarian" armies; enter "Save Darfur!" and, voila!, a movement is born. Seventh: continue to chip away the power of the enemy by chipping away at their credibility. Eighth: under the banners of high moral approbation, and with full support of a deeply caring Western public, overthrow the malevolent forces (of Islam and the Orient) and instill a benevolent, peace-loving, pro-democracy government. Last: wipe away the sanctions, no longer needed, and bring much-needed "development" to another backward country. And there you have it: yet another *civilizing* mission to conquer those barbaric Arab hoardes, and those starving, helpless, uneducated, diseased, tribal, Africans"[82]

Sudan, Kosovo, and Yugoslavia "illustrate the efficiency with which the opinion cartel can mobilize the public on behalf of foreign military crusades that advance the cause of world government – without even explicitly stating that world government [or One World Company] is the goal. Prior to the media's "humanitarian" propaganda campaigns, neither Somalia nor Kosovo figured prominently among the typical American's concerns"[83]

The same could be said for the first Gulf War. 87% of Americans couldn't find Iraq on a map and had no idea who Saddam Hussein was until CFR-run CNN's "diligent, relentless efforts to indoctrinate the [American] public made those military campaigns possible."[84] By the end of 2010, more than one and a half million Iraqis were dead, along with Saddam Hussein and 5,000+ American troops who are "liberating" the country on behalf of British Petroleum, Royal Dutch Shell, Halliburton, Blackwater, Chase Manhattan Bank, Bank of America, CitiGroup and an unending procession of multinational corporations, all vying for a piece of the Iraqi sweepstakes.

"In a sense, the "news" media generally tell one story: The saga of Government as Savior. On nearly every conceivable issue, domestic or foreign, news stories are designed to encourage readers and viewers to look to government intervention as a solution.... The Establishment media are conscious, willing accomplices in the power elite's drive for global control. To control the world, the power elite must conquer the public mind."[85] As Walter Lippmann said: "News and the truth are not the same thing..."

ONE ELITE, MANY CONDUITS

Many Americans still persist in believing that we have a free press, while getting most of their news from coporate-controlled television, under the misconception that reporters are meant to serve the public. "Reporters are paid employees and serve the media owners,"[86] whose companies' shares are traded on Wall Street.

"If you've recently watched the nightly news or prime-time TV, bought a best-selling book, picked up a "local" newspaper, bought a CD, or attended a movie, chances are that the product in question has passed through a CFR-connected corporate filter."In January 2001, a $165 billion merger joined America Online (AOL), the world's largest Internet service provider, with Time Warner, creating history's largest news, entertainment, and publishing conglomerate. The key players in the merger were Gerald Levin and W. Thomas Johnson, both of whom are members of the

CFR. Even a cursory review of the corporate rolls of AOL Time Warner and its CNN news subsidiary demonstrates that the CFR essentially runs both operations.

> Both AOL Time Warner and Disney/ABC are CFR corporate members, and together they control more than $200 billion in news and entertainment assets. Vivendi Universal and Sony round out the global media-entertainment complex, accounting for large chunks of the movie and music industry. Both Vivendi and Sony's American subsidiary are corporate CFR members.[87]

In turn, "the Rockefellers have an important stake as shareholders of several US corporate media;"[88] the same corporate media with links to the US foreign policy-national security-intelligence establishment that today is working closely with the supposed anti-establishment WikiLeaks on redacting, distribution and dissemination to the public of secret documents. Again and again, as the evidence mounts, I keep coming back to the same question. Is there something wrong with the picture?

THE ROLE OF THE CORPORATE MEDIA

"WikiLeaks was started up in December 2006. Oddly enough, as a supposed 'leak' site, a dissident site, it was given a great deal of immediate mainstream attention from the likes of the *Washington Post, Time* magazine, and even Cass Sunstein, the now Obama administration official who wrote a paper on how to 'cognitively infiltrate' dissident groups in order to steer them in a direction that is useful to the powers that be."[89]

Scott Creighton makes a great point in his December 11, 2010 globalresearch.ca article. "The *Time* magazine article is curious because it seems that right off the bat they were telling us how to interpret WikiLeaks in such a way that sounded strangely familiar to George W. Bush back just after 9/11..."[90]

This is what a real world would look like if only what we are being told by *Time* magazine was written for the benefit of the readers instead of it being a cheap trick to convince the unaware masses of WikiLeaks real agenda. "By March, more than one million leaked documents from governments and corporations in Asia, the Middle East, sub-Saharan Africa and the former Soviet Bloc will be available online in a bold new collective experiment in whistle-blowing. That is, of course, as long as you don't accept any of the conspiracy theories brewing that WikiLeaks.org could be a front for the CIA or some other intelligence agency."[91]

Continuing from Creighton, "Now remember and read closely ... this article was written before WikiLeaks' first big 'leak', which according to the article was to occur sometime in March of 2007.

> So why would *Time* magazine be writing about them in the first place if they hadn't done anything yet? [Why are they going out on a limb in a such a risky way, unless of course they know something we don't.] Also, let's not pass up on that delicious irony: this is *Time* magazine singing the praises of a supposed 'leak' site which will supposedly expose all kinds of 'conspiracy theories' while at the same time telling their readers NOT to believe in those silly 'conspiracy theories' circulating about WikiLeaks. Just so long as you believe the 'correct' conspiracy theories, you'll be all right I guess. This of course perfectly matches Julian Assange's own statements about 9/11.[92]

But, we will get to that.

Now, read the following from *Time*: "Instead of a couple of academic specialists, WikiLeaks will provide a forum for the entire global community to examine any document relentlessly for credibility, plausibility, veracity and falsifiability, its organizers write on the site's FAQ page."[93]

Quoting Time some more: "They will be able to interpret documents and explain their relevance to the public. If a document is leaked from the Chinese government, the entire Chinese dissident community can freely scrutinize and discuss it…"[94] Does this sound like a public relations propaganda piece written by the boys on Madison Avenue?

Sounds like a WikiLeaks "How To" guide. Please understand you are being told what to think and how to interpret the information. Of course, in order to interpret it 'correctly' you must have the right mindset. But, in order to get the unsuspecting public into the right mindset, WikiLeaks needed the official blessing of the leading mainstream corporate media publications. Without the public's support, this little project looked doomed to fail before it even got off the ground. Is that why Rupert Murdoch's public relations guy was on the board of directors of WikiLeaks? Is that the reason both *Time* magazine and the *Washington Post* had to come out with supportive articles about WikiLeaks before anyone knew anything about them?

"This collaboration between WikiLeaks and selected mainstream media is not fortuitous; it was part of an agreement between several major US and European newspapers [*The New York Times* (Bilderberg, CFR), the *Guardian* (the left wing of the British intelligence agencies), *Der Spiegel* (Bilderberg) and to a lesser degree with the London *Economist* (Bilderberg)] and WikiLeaks' editor Julian Assange."[95] These large corporations are "directly involved in the editing and selection of leaked documents."[96] In other words, the press and Assange are partners.

"WikiLeaks and The Economist have also entered into what seems to be a contradictory relationship. WikiLeaks founder and editor Julian Assange was granted in 2008 The Economist's New Media Award."[97] Yet, another coincidence, I'll bet.

"The *Economist* has a close relationship to Britain's financial elites."[98] "The *Economist* started publishing in the heyday of the British East India Empire in 1843; that it intervened regularly in American politics, including against Abraham Lincoln's efforts to save the Union; and that it today represents everything which is the antithesis of the American Revolution."[99]

> It is an establishment news outlet, which has, on balance, supported Britain's involvement in the Iraq war. *The Economist's* Editor-in-Chief, John Micklethwait was a participant in eight of the last ten Bilderberg conferences.
>
> *The Economist* is jointly owned by Britain's Rothschild family and Lazard Frères banking houses, both close to Britain's royal family. "Sir Evelyn Robert Adrian de Rothschild was chairman of *The Economist* from 1972 to 1989. His wife Lynn Forester de Rothschild currently sits on *The Economist's* board. The Rothschild family also has a sizeable shareholder interest in *The Economist*. Former Editor of *The Economist* (1974-86), Andrew Stephen Bower Knight is currently Chairman of the J. Rothschild Capital Management Fund. He is also reported to have been member of the Steering Group (1986) of the Bilderberg.[100]

Lazard is a leading French and British asset of the Anglo-Dutch combine, centered in Royal Dutch Shell [the Dutch and the British Royal families] and in the Rothschild banking organization."[101] This is the phenomenon called the Bilderberg Group. "Hyppolyte Worms, the founder of Banque Worms, [itself a creation of Lazard,] was a shipping magnate, whose business was built on its contracts to deliver Royal Dutch Shell oil. He was also one of the 12 founding members of the Synarchist Movement of Empires, the secret organization behind the delivery of France over to Hitler and the Nazis. Lazard Fréres was the French investment bank for Shell, and it was in that capacity that Lazard was instrumental in the creation of the banking arm of the Worms group, Banque Worms et Cie."[102]

As Chossudovsky correctly asks in his globalresearch.ca article, "why would Julian Assange receive the support from Britain's foremost establishment news outfit that has consistently been involved in media disinformation"[103] and with clearly defined links to Anglo-Dutch Royalty, the Bilderberg group and the Rothschild banking family?

> Are we not dealing with a case of 'manufactured dissent', whereby the process of supporting and rewarding WikiLeaks for its endeavors, becomes a means of controlling and manipulating the WikiLeaks project, while at the same time embedding it into the mainstream media?
> It is also worth mentioning another important link. Julian Assange's lawyer Mark Stephens of Finers Stephens Innocent (FSI), a major London elite law firm, happens to be the legal adviser to the Rothschild Waddesdon Trust. While this in itself does not prove anything, it should nonetheless be examined in the broader context of WikiLeaks' social and corporate entourage: the NYT, the CFR, the Bilderberg group, *The Economist*, *Time* magazine, *Forbes*, Finers Stephens Innocent (FSI), etc.[104]

WikiLeaks Corporate Entourage

The important question is, who is behind the entire process of selection, distribution and editing of released documents to the broader public? What US foreign policy objectives are being served through this redacting process?

"Is WikiLeaks part of an awakening of public opinion, of a battle against the lies and fabrications, which appear daily in the print media and on network TV?"[105] Or is it a part of a process of infiltrating alternative media, critical of the government's way of handling the US foreign policy? How can this battle against media disinformation be waged with the participation and collaboration of the corporate architects of media disinformation?

With the *New York Times/the Guardian/Der Spiegel/ The Economist* "WikiLeaks has enlisted the architects of media disinformation to fight media disinformation: An incongruous and self-defeating procedure."[106] ... especially in light of past media transgressions.

OPERATION MOCKINGBIRD

Starting in the early days of the Cold War (late 40s), the CIA began a secret project called Operation Mockingbird, an initiative of the CIA's Office of Special Projects (OSP). *Virtual Government*, author Alex Constantine explains it as a "CIA project designed to influence the major media for domestic propaganda purposes." Washington Post reporter, Carl Bernstein – who came to fame with his colleague Bob Woodward, for their exposé of the Nixon administration's illegal re-election campaign activities, known as "Watergate" – dropped a media bombshell on an unsuspecting America.

In an October 1977 article published by *Rolling Stone* magazine, Bernstein reported that more than 400 American journalists worked for the CIA. Bernstein went on to reveal that this cozy arrangement had covered the preceding 25 years. Sources told Bernstein that the New York Times, America's most respected newspaper at the time, was one of the CIA's closest media collaborators. Seeking to spread the blame, the New York Times published an article in December 1977, revealing that "more than eight hundred news and public information organizations and individuals," had participated in the CIA's covert subversion of the media.[107]

These "collaborators," provided the CIA with direct access to a large number of newspapers and magazines, scores of news services and press agencies such as Reuters and the Associated Press, radio and television as well as Hollywood studios. Media assets will eventually include ABC, NBC, CBS, Time, Newsweek, Associated Press, United Press International (UPI), Reuters, Hearst Newspapers, Scripps-Howard, Copley News Service, etc. and 400 journalists, who have secretly carried out assignments according to documents on file at CIA headquarters, from intelligence-gathering to serving as go-betweens.

The CIA had infiltrated the nation's businesses, media, and universities with tens of thousands of on-call operatives by the 1950's. CIA Director Dulles had staffed the CIA almost exclusively with Ivy League graduates, especially from Yale with figures like George Herbert Walker Bush from the "Skull and Crossbones" Society."[108]

Other luminaries of the US media subverted by the CIA included "Henry Luce, publisher of *Time* magazine, Arthur Hays Sulzberger, of the *New York Times* and C.D. Jackson of *Fortune* magazine."[109]

This information became public knowledge in 1975, as a result of the investigation by U.S. Senator Frank Church, through the Select Committee on Governmental Operations Studies on the Intelligence Agencies. The most important individual prostituting himself on behalf of the CIA was legendary journalist Walter Cronkite, a former intelligence officer himself and a paragon of journalistic virtue.

> Constantine reveals in an Internet essay.[110] Citing historian C. Vann Woodward's *New York Times* article of 1987, Ronald Reagan, later to become President of the US, was a FBI snitch earlier in his life. This dated back to the time when Reagan was President of the Actor's Guild. Woodward says that Reagan "fed the names of suspect people in his organization to the FBI secretly and regularly enough to be assigned an informer's code number, T.10." The purpose was to purge the film industry of "subversives."[111]

British investigator David Guyatt goes even further: "One journalist is worth twenty agents, a high-level source told Bernstein. Spies were trained as journalists and then later infiltrated – often with the publishers consent – into the most prestigious media outlets in America, including the *New York Times* and *Time* magazine. Likewise, numerous reputable journalists underwent training in various aspects of 'spook-craft' by the CIA. This included techniques as varied as secret writing, surveillance and other spy crafts."[112]

Speaking of journalists who sold themselves to the CIA, Phil Graham, the then owner of the *Washington Post* is said to have remarked that it was cheaper to buy a first-rate journalist than to have a one-night stand with a high-class whore.

> Of the fifty plus overseas news proprietary's owned by the CIA were *The Rome Daily American, The Manilla Times* and the *Bangkok Post.*[113]

The *Washington Post* was the key media outlet for off-the-book CIA information, and the individual chosen for the job of disinformation in the *Post* was a then-unknown Bob Woodward. Woodward's finest hour was Watergate, which toppled Richard Nixon. What is almost unknown is how the mainstream media account of Watergate was different from the one told by Bob Woodward and Carl Bernstein.

WOODWARD: THE TRUE STORY

In his publisher's forward for *Watergate Exposed*, Trine-Day's publisher Kris Millegan writes: "Bob Woodward was no ordinary news reporter, As Russ Baker, author of *Family of Secrets* states at whowhatwhy.com: 'Bob, top secret Naval officer, gets sent to work in the Nixon White House while still on military duty. Then, with no journalistic credentials to speak of, and with a boost from White House staffers, he lands a job at the *Washington Post*. Not long thereafter he starts to take down Richard Nixon. Meanwhile, Woodward's military bosses are running a spy ring inside the White House that is monitoring Nixon and Kissinger's secret negotiations with America's enemies (China, Soviet Union, etc), stealing documents and funnelling them back to the Joint Chiefs of Staff.'"

In this new book on Watergate, co-author Robert Merritt, a man without a face and the FBI's most important informant in the last half-century, reveals that the CIA conducted illegal wiretaps of all key politicians in Washington. This is the information that Woodward, over the years, has managed to use in his books to get rid of pesky politicians and other challengers that made life difficult for the Shadow

Government, the real power behind the throne described in my last book, *Shadow Masters*.

THE CIA AND THE CORPORATE MEDIA

In the words of Canadian economist, Michel Chossudovsky, "Media disinformation has become institutionalized in the XXI century. The lies and fabrications have become increasingly blatant when compared to the 1970s. The US media has become the mouthpiece of US foreign policy. Disinformation is routinely 'planted' by CIA operatives in the newsroom of major dailies, magazines and TV channels."[114] Quoting Chaim Kupferberg: "A relatively few well-connected correspondents provide the scoops, that get the coverage in the relatively few mainstream news sources, where the parameters of debate are set and the 'official reality' is consecrated for the bottom feeders in the news chain."[115]

Chossudovsky's article continues:

> Since 2001, the US media has assumed a new role in sustaining the 'Global War on Terrorism' (GWOT) and camouflaging US sponsored war crimes. In the wake of 9/11, Defense Secretary Donald Rumsfeld created the Office of Strategic Influence (OSI), or 'Office of Disinformation' as it was labelled by its critics: "The Department of Defense said they needed to do this, and they were going to actually plant stories that were false in foreign countries – as an effort to influence public opinion across the world."
>
> Today's corporate media is an instrument of war propaganda, which begs the question: why would the *New York Times* all of a sudden promote transparency and truth in media, by assisting WikiLeaks in "spreading the word"; and *that people around the world would not pause for one moment and question the basis of this incongruous relationship.* [emphasis added]
>
> ...given the corporate media's cohesive and structured relationship to US intelligence, not to mention the links

of individual journalists to the military-national security establishment, the issue of a CIA sponsored WikiLeaks PsyOp must necessarily be addressed.

WikiLeaks has the essential features of a process of 'manufactured dissent.' It seeks to expose government lies. It has released important information on US war crimes. But once the project becomes embedded in the mould of mainstream journalism, it is used as an instrument of media disinformation: 'It is in the interest of the corporate elites to accept dissent and protest as a feature of the system inasmuch as they do not threaten the established social order. The purpose is not to repress dissent, but, on the contrary, to shape and mould the protest movement, to set the outer limits of dissent. To maintain their legitimacy, the economic elites favour limited and controlled forms of opposition... To be effective, however, the process of 'manufacturing dissent' must be carefully regulated and monitored by those who are the object of the protest movement.

What this examination of the WikiLeaks project also suggests is that the mechanics of New World Order propaganda, particularly with regard to its military agenda, has become increasingly sophisticated.

It no longer relies on the outright suppression of the facts regarding US-NATO war crimes. Nor does it require that the reputation of government officials at the highest levels, including the Secretary of State, be protected. New World Order politicians are in a sense 'disposable'. They can be replaced. What must be protected and sustained are the interests of the economic elites, which control the political apparatus from behind the scenes.

In the case of WikiLeaks, the facts are contained in a data bank; many of those facts, particularly those pertaining to foreign governments serve US foreign policy interests. Other facts tend, on the other hand to discredit the US administration. That adds to the WikiLeaks standing amongst most people who believe them to be an anti-establishment organ for the truth.[116]

Again, it must be stressed that:

All the Wiki-facts are selectively redacted, they are then 'analyzed' and interpreted by a media which serves the economic elites. While the numerous pieces of information contained in the WikiLeaks data bank are accessible, the broader public will not normally take the trouble to consult and scan through the WikiLeaks data bank. The public will read the redacted selections and interpretations presented in major news outlets.

A partial and biased picture is presented. The redacted version is accepted by public opinion because it is based on what is heralded as a 'reliable source', when in fact what is presented in the pages of major newspapers and on network TV is a carefully crafted and convoluted distortion of the truth.

Limited forms of critical debate and 'transparency' are tolerated while also enforcing broad public acceptance of the basic premises of US foreign policy, including its "Global War on Terrorism." With regard to a large segment of the US antiwar movement, this strategy seems to have succeeded: 'We are against war but we support the 'war on terrorism.'[117]

Let's analyze this. The big lie of the 21st century is terrorism itself – al-Qaeda and Osama bin Laden. One can judge the validity of information by what is hidden rather than what is revealed. Does WikiLeaks say anything about bin Laden? According to the papers that Assange has released, bin Laden at the time was allegedly in Quetta, taking part in Quetta Shura, the Council of the alleged terrorist chiefs. So, the subliminal message from the government is 'we have to go into Pakistan and get him.'

According to WikiLeaks, up until his alleged death at the hands of United States SEALs, Osama bin Laden was very much alive, conveniently maintaining the myth for the American administration and its "War on Terror at a point when most Americans had forgotten the original reason the Bush Administration allegedly invaded Afghanistan."[118] Readers should recall that the supposed reason for the invasion was to go after Bin Laden as the mastermind of 9/11.

The problem with this version of events as far as bin Laden is concerned, is that all of the world's intelligence services know he died in December 2001.

"But it gets better," Scott Creighton writes. "Few of you might know that just prior to the unveiling of WikiLeaks, the intelligence world had an unveiling of their own... a 'social media' based resource called 'Intellipedia.'"

"With its own versions of a certain search engine and a certain online encyclopedia, the intelligence community is evolving its use of tools now widespread in the commercial sector, generating both success and controversy. The new tools include a federated search engine called Oogle and Intellipedia, a controversial intelligence data-sharing tool based on Wiki social software technology."[119]

Thus, back in September 2006 the intelligence community was already hard at work "on several new 'pedia' type programs on the one hand to serve as a data-base"[120] and on the other, one which would work like a Google search engine.

JULIAN ASSANGE

With thousands of pages written about him, Julian Assange has suddenly become a bright light of truth as a result of his spectacular media coup. WikiLeaks has apparently placed nearly every country in the world in an uncomfortable position. No nation has been spared embarrassment – not governments nor intelligence agencies or top bosses of the world's large multinationals. Drug traffickers, weapons dealers, diamond traders, terrorists, businessmen, clergy and Obama's government officials fear revelations from a man who, until very recently, was a complete unknown. But who is he? Where did he come from? Assange seems to have materialized out of nowhere. No past, no history.

When the WikiLeaks phenomenon appeared on the scene, the Russian government, according to sources close to the President, had committed a large contingent of agents to crack the Assange riddle. The British MI6 is dipping into its emergency budget to discover the identity of leakers. It is not often that so many governments and intelligence agencies have devoted so many of their resources and efforts to unearth the truth about one person.

Sources at the NSA, America's largest spy agency, place Assange in Hamburg during the first Gulf War. Russian intelligence services, instead, place him at a cyber hacker party in Singapore in October 1986. CIA sources, however, are convinced that Assange has been recruited by several intelligence agencies, including the Israeli Mossad, through a Jewish computer scientist at the University of Melbourne, who was involved with the community of hackers and simultaneously worked for the Israeli Mossad.

There is little reliable data on Assange. He is supposedly 40 years old, but if he works for some of the intelligence agencies as their front man, we can be sure that his 'urban legend' is built on a healthy dose of smoke and mirrors. What little is known about him, is that Assange is a super-hacker associated with Chaos Computer Club in Hamburg, Germany in the late 1980s. The leader of the group, Karl Koch was a legendary hacker who invented a famous Trojan virus that destroyed many of the U.S. government's military computers. At that time, Koch was already in the crosshairs of German intelligence because he was trying to sell the operating system source code to the Soviet KGB.

In what is considered to have been one of the biggest espionage scandals of the time, five West German hackers sold military and economic intelligence to the Soviet Union after infiltrating secret data networks, such as U.S. nuclear weapons lab in Los Alamos, home of NASA, the databases of the U.S. military, as well as the database OPTIMIS of the Joint Chiefs of Staff. In Europe, the same hackers cracked the network of Franco-Italian arms manufacturer Thomson, European Space Agency ESA, the Max Planck Institute for

Nuclear Physics in Heidelberg, CERN in Geneva and Germany's DESY electron accelerator in Hamburg.

This was done on behalf of the Soviet KGB during a period of three years, in return for sums of between $50,000 and $100,000, as well as drugs. The Soviets received five disks with secret information between May and December 1986, at an undisclosed location in East Berlin. These discs contained thousands of passwords and computer codes, access mechanisms and programs that allowed the Soviet Union access to computer centers in the Western world.

The story began back in November 1985, when Koch, self-proclaimed leader of the Chaos Computer Club, was approached by a female KGB officer who offered him the opportunity to have a lifestyle of luxury in exchange for 'hacker knowledge.'

At the time, German government spokesmen agreed that this was the most serious espionage case in West Germany since Guenter Guillaume was unmasked in 1974. Guillaume, a senior aide to West Germany's Chancellor Willy Brandt, turned out to be an East German spy.

For many people within the underworld of computer hackers, Karl Koch, alias Hagbard, was a genius, a visionary who spent most of his short life fighting personal demons and ghosts. Many consider him the inventor of the Trojan virus, at the time an unknown cyber enemy, capable of breeching the supposedly impenetrable defenses of American and European security agencies. Koch, extremely paranoid even before he became a cocaine addict, would later sell the priceless information to the Soviet KGB in the last days of the Cold War. His mother died of cancer in 1976. His father, an alcoholic, could hardly serve as a role model for Koch. To escape from real life, Koch crossed into the parallel world of the *Illuminati Trilogy* by Robert Anton Wilson and Robert Shea, a strange mix of conspiracy theories and secret societies, reality and fiction. In fact, his nickname was the name of a character in the book.

According to sources in the KGB, in mid-1986, Karl Koch told several friends at a hacker party that he was offered a hard-to-turn-down deal that would solve his financial problems. One of those present according to the Federal Security Service of the Russian Federation (FSB), was the founder of WikiLeaks, Julian Assange. Another individual whose name appears in the archives of the KGB is the programmer Dirk Brezinski of West Berlin. KGB reports describe Brezinski as a computer genius who worked part time for the mainframe operating system, Siemens – BS-2000.

According to KGB intelligence, Dirk Brezinski and Assange met in Singapore in 1994. Over time, Assange became one of the most recognizable faces on the Planet. Koch wasn't so lucky. He died on May 23, 1989 when police found his badly burned body, covered in tattoos and phallic symbols, in a forest near Gifhorn. The police report speaks of suicide, but with Koch's background, many speculate that it was a terrible payback by someone linked to an intelligence agency.

However, the list of hackers with links to secret service agencies, interlocked objectives, triple agents and long-range government agendas gets even wackier. "It is no secret that hackers are often recruited by governmental authorities for cyber security purposes."[121] KGB recruiting of Karl Koch is just one example. Peiter Zatko a.k.a. "Mudge" is another individual existing in this lunatic fringe. In an interview with *Forbes* magazine, Assange made the following observations regarding his connection to Peiter Zatko:

> Assange: Yeah, I know Mudge. He's a very sharp guy.
>
> Greenberg (*Forbes*): Mudge is now leading a project at the Pentagon's Defense Advanced Research Projects Agency to find a technology that can stop leaks, which seems pretty relative [sic] to your organization. Can you tell me about your past relationship with Mudge?
>
> Assange: Well, I... no comment.

Greenberg: Were you part of the same scene of hackers? When you were a computer hacker, you must have known him well.

Assange: We were in the same milieu. I spoke with everyone in that milieu.

Greenberg: What do you think of his current work to prevent digital leaks inside of organizations, a project called Cyber Insider Threat or Cinder?

Assange: I know nothing about it.[122]

Let's see if we can help Julian Assange remember. Business Wire's February 1, 2005 article on the subject is candid and largely on target. It is quoted by Julie Lévesque in his *Who's Who at WikiLeaks*? "Peiter Zatko is an expert in cyber warfare. He worked for BBN Technolgies (a subsidiary of Raytheon) with engineers who perform leading edge research and development to protect Department of Defense data... Mr. Zatko is focused on anticipating and protecting against the next generation of information and network security threats to government and commercial networks."[123] Lévesque's article continued:

In another *Forbes* interview, we learn that Mr. Zatko is 'a lead cybersecurity researcher at the Defense Advanced Research Projects Agency [DARPA], the mad-scientist wing of the Pentagon.' His project 'aims to rid the world of digital leaks.'

There also seems to be a connection between Zatko and former hacker Jacob Appelbaum, a WikiLeaks spokesperson. Zatko and Appelbaum were purportedly part of a hacker group called Cult of the Dead Cow. Appelbaum currently works for the Tor Project, a United States Naval Research Laboratory initiative. The sponsors of that project listed on its website are:

NLnet Foundation (2008-2009), Naval Research Laboratory (2006-2010), an anonymous North American ISP (2009-2010), provided up to $100k. Google (2008-2009), Google Summer of Code (2007-2009), Human Rights

Watch (George Soros' organization), Torfox (2009) and Shinjiru Technology (2009-2010) gave in turn up to $50k.

Past sponsors includes: Electronic Frontier Foundation (2004-2005), DARPA and ONR via Naval Research Laboratory (2001-2006), Cyber-TA project (2006-2008), Bell Security Solutions Inc (2006), Omidyar Network Enzyme Grant (2006), NSF via Rice University (2006-2007).

Zatko and Assange know each other. Jacob Appelbaum also played a role at WikiLeaks.[124]

Assange is linked to Chaos Computer Club through Dirk Brezinski, who is linked to the KGB through Karl Koch. The various connections tell us something regarding Assange's entourage.

I have left the best for last. From the *Forbes* interview, "we know that Mr. Zatko is a lead cybersecurity researcher at the Defense Advanced Research Projects Agency [DARPA]." So, what is DARPA?

According to DARPA's own web page, it's mission "is to maintain the technological superiority of the U.S. military and prevent technological surprise from harming our national security by sponsoring revolutionary, high-payoff research bridging the gap between fundamental discoveries and their military use."[125]

However, delving deeper, we find DARPA involved in development of a frightening technology with horrific implications. An August 3, 2003 *Boston Globe* story specifically discussed, "Defence Department funding brain-machine work." In it the writer states, "It does not take much imagination to see in this the makings of a "Matrix"-like cyberpunk dystopia: chips that impose false memories, machines that scan for wayward thoughts, cognitively augmented government security forces that impose a ruthless order on a recalcitrant population."[126] Back in the 1950s, "DARPA was the dominant sponsor of computer-related research. Cold War-driven projects like SAGE (Semi Automatic Ground Environment), an automated air-defence network of unmanned jet planes, led to a growing interest in war gaming and command systems studies."[127] Behavioral psychologist J.C.R. Licklider hoped that:

> In not too many years, human brains and computing machines will be coupled together very tightly, and that the resulting partnership will think as no human brain has ever thought and process data in a way not approached by the information-handling machines we know today.
>
> That hope would take form in such later projects as DARPA's Augmented Cognition (Aug-Cog) to create soldier-computer 'dyads,' and the movement for a 'Post-Human Renaissance,' where 'there are no demarcations between bodily existence and computer simulation, between cybernetic mechanism and biological organism. This would become the Holy Grail of the front-end research that has spun off not only future battlefield technologies, but also much of today's video game industry.[128]

The 2007 article titled "Video Games and the Wars of the Future" explains this phenomenon in no uncertain terms:

> A 1997 report entitled 'Modeling and Simulation: Linking Entertainment and Defense,' summarized the proceedings of a National Research Council conference which brought together representatives from the military and entertainment world. Their goal was to map out a working relationship whereby the same cutting-edge simulations and virtual reality research brought to bear on enhanced training programs for the military, could also be used in commercially developed video games. Such would be the mission of the Institute for Creative Technologies (ICT).
>
> ...the ultimate aim, explicitly outlined by some of ICT's creators, is to actually construct Star Trek's 'holodeck' (the holographic simulations room used on the TV show), ...whose research includes the role of video-game play on performance in simulated environments: 'Recent neurobiological studies have found that emotional experiences stimulate mechanisms that enhance the creation of long-term memories. Thus, more effective training scenarios can be designed by incorporating key emotional cues.' Creating memories is exactly what simulation

research is all about, according to West Point graduate Michael Macedonia, the chief scientist and technical director of PEO STRI who helped create the ICT....

The training techniques being designed by today's "visionaries" in virtual technologies and artificial intelligence are, in reality, based on nothing more than the reductionist belief that the human mind is a programmable system, not fundamentally different from an animal or machine. The age of cyborgs, according to DARPA and ICT is just around the corner.[129]

And this is exactly the "religion" that Julian Assange and his haphazard crew have been peddling since the inception of the project known as WikiLeaks.

MIRROR, MIRROR ON THE WALL

Then there is Assange the author. As investigative journalist Julie Lévesque explained in globalresearch on December 20, 2010: "In ... *Underground: Hacking, Madness and Obsession on the Electronic Frontier* (1997) ... From the start, Assange states that he undertook the research for the book; however, he fails to mention that he was actually one of the hackers analyzed in the book," going by the name of Mendax, a Latin word for "'lying, false....'"[130]

Also, according to former NSA intelligence agent and investigative journalist Wayne Madsen, Assange claims to be a PhD. But "Asian intelligence sources point out that Assange's "PhD" is from Moffett University, an on-line diploma mill that dispatches university degrees for a fee. At the beginning of his career, he claimed to come from Nairobi, Kenya, when he actually is from Australia where his exploits have included computer hacking and software piracy."[131]

WikiLeaks purports to protect all leakers' identities and have the most stringent security and/or privacy policy for the Internet in place, which cyber security experts all agree to be blatantly false. In February 2011, Reuters reported that "WikiLeaks' ability to receive new leaks has been crippled after a disaffected programmer unplugged a component which guaranteed anonymity to would-be leakers,"[132] implying that the inability was caused by a disaffected former employee.

Nice deception, but not true. Cryptome.org, "the site set up to publish information about communications security,"[133] released a series of lawful spying guides to internet service providers which show how they co-operate with law enforcement and government and each other in gathering information on their users, for commercial and governmental purposes.

What does this information tell the public? It shows that privacy policies put up by Internet providers and web sites are completely phony and deceptive. "There is no such thing as privacy on the Internet," candidly states Cryptome's founder John Young in an interview on *The Brian Lehrer TV Show*. "The data collection begins with you signing up to the Internet. If you have been on it for at least a year, there is nothing about you that is not known."[134]

> There is none that is not superficial and illusory. Security and/or privacy policy for the Internet and digital communication are unbelievable. Digital communication should be seen as a spying machine. The Internet is a magnificently appealing means to gather data on its bewitched users – for harvesting by governments, commerce, institutions and individuals, but especially by the providers of Internet services, distribution systems and equipment.[135]

Does it mean that if the Internet service provider knows it, so does the government?

> "Yes it does," says John Young, Cryptome's founder in the aforementioned Brian Lehrer interview. "All this data is accessible to these authoritative institutions. They share it amongst themselves. That is what the Internet is used for. It is a vast spying machine."

Assange also claims that he can protect WikiLeaks from being taken down by basing it in a country that can and will protect it.

"Not so," says Young. "There is no place where a take-down cannot occur. The distribution system for communication can always be blocked and servers confiscated. Only multiple, growing and changing public outlets for prohibited information can offer a chance of avoiding shutdown, demonization, corruption through finance and bribery and orchestrated distrust."[136]

A pattern emerges. A pattern of deception and lies and double-speak of intelligence agencies and their black operations hidden behind once or twice-removed deniable cut-outs. Julian Assange. WikiLeaks project. The CIA. The NSA. Google. Soros.

In *Underground: Hacking, Madness and Obsession on the Electronic Frontier*, Assange begins with the following Oscar Wilde quote: "Man is least himself when he talks in his own person. Give him a mask, and he will tell you the truth." And this quote from a French writer Antoine De Saint-Exupery, best remembered for his novella *The Little Prince*: "What is essential is invisible to the eye."

Although it is impossible to confirm that the above quotes were self refernces, they nonetheless suggest that Assange, at the time, may have been hiding his true identity.[137]

THE MONEY TRAIL

One of the obvious questions about Assange is, who pays him? If we follow the money, we fairly quickly come to a dead end. Who pays for this lifestyle that he has? On the one hand, we are told he is a nomad, a sort of elite hobo, someone who jet-sets around the world with a duffel bag full of socks, living out of a backpack, sleeping on office floors, showing up in different parts of the world. This is surely not a typical profile of a happy-go-lucky young man. Rather, it is a profile of a spy, or rather a picaresque agent.

Scott Creighton's January 1, 2011, blog-post succinctly tells the story: "Julian is probably the only anti-establishment dissident that I know of currently hanging out on the multi-million dollar estate of an establishment blue-blood with connections to George Soros. Assange spent a lovely Christmas holiday in Ellington Hall, the estate of Vaughan Smith, the man who owns and operates the Frontline Club. International globalist, Bilderberg member and speculator extraordinaire, George Soros, helped Smith set up the Frontline Club. When you consider that every single 'WikiLeak' released to this day does nothing except build support for globalist agendas, this connection seems beyond obvious in its implications."[138]

John Young is a founder of Cryptome.org, a whistleblower site. He "began publishing documents in 1996, incurring the wrath of UK and US governments. The archive endures. Young was invited to be the 'public face' of WikiLeaks at the formation of the venture, but declined."[139]

In an email to John Young, one WikiLeaks insider also raises the question of Assange's credibility: "Julian Assange's very public fund raising campaign has effectively stalled with past and potential investors fading into the background. As previously indicated it is NOT the philosophy of WikiLeaks that is in question, but Assange's credibility."[140]

While demanding 'transparency' from governments and corporations around the world, Assange is indeed very secretive when it comes to revealing his personal biography and his former business associates prior to launching the WikiLeaks project.

His bio states that he is a "prolific programmer and consultant for many open-source projects and his software is used by most large organizations and is inside every Apple computer."[141] Was he working freelance? Who did he work for? Does Apple know he was working for them? Apple is certainly denying it. Is this like his PhD from a phantom on-line university? Or is it simply his narcissistic fixation dominating his personality?

The lack of transparency again creeps into Assange's personal dealings. Who is he, really? An old email exchange from

1994 between Julian Assange and NASA award winner Fred Blonder raises questions regarding Assange's professional activities prior to launching WikiLeaks. This exchange is available on the website of the Massachusetts Institute of Technology:[142]

> Date: Fri, 18 Nov 1994 03:59:19 +0100
> From: Julian Assange <proff@suburbia.apana.org.au>
> To: Fred Blonder <fred@nasirc.hq.nasa.gov>
> Cc: karl@bagpuss.demon.co.uk, Quentin.Fennessy@sematech.
> org,
> fred@nasirc.hq.nasa.gov, mcn@c3serve.c3.lanl.gov, bugtraq@
> fc.net
> In-Reply-To: <199411171611.LAA04177@nasirc.hq.nasa.gov>
> On Thu, 17 Nov 1994, Fred Blonder wrote: [EXCERPT]
>
> > From: Julian Assange <proff@suburbia.apana.org.au>
> >
> > .
> > Of course, to make things really interesting, we could have n files,
> > comprised of n-1 setuid/setgid scripts and 1 setuid/setgid binary, with
> > each script calling the next as its #! argument and the last calling the
> > binary. ;-)
> >
> > The '#!' exec-hack does not work recursively. I just tried it under SunOs 4.1.3
> > It generated no diagnostics and exited with status 0, but it also didn't execute
> > the target binary....
> > Proff

"Julian Assange's e-mail to Fred Blonder was sent to an address ending with 'nasirc.hq.nasa.gov', namely NASA. The e-mail was also sent (cc) to Michael C. Neuman, a computer expert at Los Alamos National Laboratory (LANL), New Mexico, a premier national security research institution, under the jurisdiction of the US Department of Energy.

"At the time, Fred Blonder was working on a cyber security program called 'NASA Automated Systems Incident Response Capability' (NASIRC), for which he won the NASA Group Achievement Award in 1995. A report from June 2, 1995 explains:

NASIRC has significantly elevated agency-wide awareness of serious evolving threats to NASA's computer/ network systems through on-going threat awareness briefings and in-depth technical workshop sessions and through intercenter communications and cooperation relating to the responsive and timely sharing of incident information and tools and techniques.[143]

"For example, in his e-mail, Assange updates Blonder on his work, referring to 'other platforms I have not as yet tested', seemingly indicating that he was collaborating with the NASA employee. One thing we can confirm is that Julian Assange was in communication with people working for NASA and the Los Alamos Lab in the 1990s....

"On the list of board members published previously by WikiLeaks, we can read that Julian Assange:

• has 'attended 37 schools and 6 universities', none of which are mentioned by name;
• is 'Australia's most famous ethical computer hacker'. A court case from 1996 cited abundantly in the mainstream press is available on the Australasian Legal Information Institute. Contrary to all the other cases listed on the afore-mentioned link, the full text of Assange's case is not available;
• 'in the first prosecution of its type... [he] defended a case in the supreme court for his role as the editor of an activist electronic magazine'. The name of the magazine, the year of the prosecution, the country where it took place are not mentioned;
• allegedly founded 'Pickup' civil rights group for children'. No information about this group seems to be available, other than in reports related to WikiLeaks. We don't know if it still exists, where it is located and what are its activities.

- 'studied mathematics, philosophy and neuroscience.' We don't know where he studied or what his credentials are;
- 'has been a subject of several books and documentaries.' If so, why not mention at least one of them?

"Is there any relation between Assange's prosecution for hacking in 1996 and this exchange? Was he collaborating with these institutions?"[144] If he was, then Assange is a once removable, deniable cut out. Part of an off-the-book secret government run operations. "Some people suspect that this is a false flag operation intended to control the Internet."[145]

What we do know is that his parents ran a travelling theatre company in Australia. *New Yorker* reporter Raffi Khatchadourian delves deep into Assange's past and we learn about the abbreviated childhood that shaped his obsessions. Assange lived for a time on tiny Magnetic Island off the coast of Australia. He was home-schooled, grew up riding horses and making rafts, and when he was eight his mom hooked up with a musician. Things got weird: "The musician became abusive, she says, and they separated. A fight ensued over the custody of Assange's half-brother, and Claire felt threatened, fearing that the musician would take away her son. Assange recalled her saying, 'Now we need to disappear,' and he lived on the run with her from the age of eleven to sixteen. When I asked him about the experience, he told me that there was evidence that the man belonged to a powerful cult called the Family-its motto was 'Unseen, Unknown, and Unheard.' Some members were doctors who persuaded mothers to give up their newborn children to the cult's leader, Anne Hamilton-Byrne. The cult had moles in government, Assange suspected, who provided the musician with leads on Claire's whereabouts."[146]

Is this Assange's paranoia or is there substance to his madness?

What is left unsaid in *The New Yorker* article is that the musician, in fact, belonged to the Anne Hamilton-Byrne cult, "which is a group of people around Melbourne, Australia who were using LSD as a treatment for children, they called therapy. The therapy consisted of giving a child LSD and locking them up in a dark room."[147]

All of this is a classic cover for intelligence agency mind-control program. Some point to an alleged infamous CIA-run operation called Project Monarch, which was imported from Nazi Germany under its old name, Marionette Programming. "Project Monarch is a U.S. Defense Department code name assigned to a subsection of the Central Intelligence Agency's double top secret projects. It is a genealogical approach to define transgenerational (via genetic psychology) behavioral modification through trauma based psychological mind control, especially in children."[148]

> The basic component of the Monarch program is the sophisticated manipulation of the mind, using extreme trauma to induce Multiple Personality Disorder. The original documentation on the project came from the Nazi SS Top Secret ("BLACK ARTS") research which the U.S. government acquired at the end of World War II and subsequently renamed, US Department of Defense's Project 63.[149]

In public testimony submitted to the President's Committee on Radiation, there are amazing allegations of severe torture foisted on Canadian, American, British and Australian children. These same children were used in radiation experiments. They detail the drug and traumatic methodology of sophisticated mind control as part of the CIA's MK-ULTRA program.[150]

Author Peter Levenda, in his extraordinary trilogy, *Sinister Forces* writes that:

> During the Watergate era a somewhat unsettling revelation was made: that for twenty-five years (or more) the CIA had conducted psychological experimentation upon both volunteers and unwitting subjects – both at home and abroad – to find the key to the unconscious mind,

to memory, and to volition. An U.S. government agency was conducting what – to a medievalist – could only be characterized as a search for the Philosopher's Stone, for occult power, for magical spells and talismans. Indeed, some of the CIA's subprojects included research among the psychics, the mediums, the magicians and the witches of America and beyond. And the Army was not far behind in its mind control testing, either.

What was even more disturbing was the revelation that nearly all records of this incredible and superhumanly ambitious project were destroyed in 1973 on orders of the CIA director Richard Helms himself. In his testimony, he claimed that MK-ULTRA did not come up with anything worthwhile, and that the project had been terminated. Then, why were the documents shredded?

We don't know who the test subjects were. We don't know what was done to them. We don't know how they have been programmed. We don't know what they might do. Or what they have done already.

We do know, however, that some of America's more colorful criminals have spent time at the same institutions receiving CIA MK-ULTRA funding for this 'special testing.' People like Charles Manson and Henry Lee Lucas, as well as 'Cinque,' the leader of the Symbionese Liberation Army that kidnapped heiress Patty Hearst.[151]

While trying to make sense of the WikiLeaks lunacy, I realized that I was standing at a nexus of history and culture: Charles Manson, the unsolved murder of hacker Karl Koch, mind control experiments…and I wondered what Australian cults, American hackers, movie stars and spies, witches and prestigious foundations, Washington and occultists, al-Qaeda and drugs, bin Laden and Julian Assange, had to do with any of it.

BLUE BEAM OF HAPPINESS

More from Levenda:

Probably only the Nazi aberration known as the Ahnenerbe-SS comes close to duplicating in scope what

MK-ULTRA was designed to do. In the former case, departments were created within Himmler's SS to research everything from the Holy Grail, mystical runes to Icelandic sagas and the World Ice Theory. In the case of MK-ULTRA, the focus was narrower at first, but soon expanded to include psychic phenomena, shamanism, remote viewing, and occult practices."[152]

Our culture in the West – formed as it is by a faith in science, a reliance on the technological – has convinced us to ignore the unseen. There is a web of connections between visible events and visible, measurable phenomena that we cannot see, cannot measure – so our response has been to ignore this web in favor of what we can see and measure. The blind leading the blind. The drunk looking for his keys under the lamppost because the light is better there.[153]

For intelligence purposes, what was required of MK-ULTRA was the ability to manipulate memory. Thus, what the Freudians call the 'superego' had to be bypassed, allowing the controller direct access to the contents of an enemy agent's mind. That was step one. Step two would involve erasing specific pieces of information from the subject's memory and replacing those pieces with new bits of memory, thus permitting the Agency to send that agent back into the field without any knowledge that he or she had been interrogated and had given up sensitive information. Step three: Could that enemy agent then be 'programmed' to commit acts on behalf of the Agency, without knowing who gave the commands or why? [Imagine the perfect spy, the perfect double agent, or even the perfect assassin.] This was the essence of the Manchurian Candidate. It is also the essence of what we know today as hypnotherapy and 'depth' psychoanalysis, for the psychotherapist looking for access to the patient's unconscious layers.... What the Agency was looking for was a key that would unlock these secrets and allow unfettered access to the human mind, with or without the volunteer cooperation from the patient.[154]

CIA director, Allen Dulles made a speech at Princeton University in April 1953, in which he "characterized the Cold War as a Manichean struggle between the forces of Light and Darkness. This was not a war over land or resources; it was a war over possession of the soul of humanity."[155]

Over the years, the CIA perfected the tests and invented a bunch of new ones, with the ostensible purpose of healing the insane. Then, CIA mind control specialists like Dr. Ewen Cameron used it to drive otherwise sane people out of their minds. Cameron believed that, "Every person is the ultimate arbiter of justice in their own conscience."

In a January 3, 2007 email to his associates, Assange gives a list of talking points to be discussed in the press and a few lines of personal observations on each point. In point 1, he states the following:

> Corporate media will shy away from or distort nuanced arguments. Need to make a few clear points and hold to them. I suggest the following, as a start, all up for discussion. (In particular, we could be more specific, or more vague about details.)
>
> 1. Ethics. We favour, and uphold, ethical behavior in all circumstances. We do not believe in unquestioning obedience to authority in all circumstances. Every person is the ultimate arbiter of justice in their own conscience. Where injustice reigns and is enshrined in law, there is a place for principled civil disobedience.[156]

Now, this may be a mere coincidence, but given the circumstances, I have my doubts. Or is it an intentional slip, an acknowledgement that he knows far more than he lets on, and perhaps even a warning to his enemies, who subjected him to such inhumane and indescribable suffering?

More clues abound that can help us understand the hidden world of Julian Assange. Towards the late 1950s, the CIA turned their considerable resources and talents towards sensory deprivation.

The idea is to completely isolate a person from his environment: have him float in water that is the same temperature as his body so there is no physical sensation, with goggles blocking all vision and earmuffs blocking all sound. With no external information source, the mind begins to turn on itself for data.... After a short time, everyone begins to hallucinate.... Not many subjects lasted more than a few hours.... According to the experts, even the strongest-willed, most adaptable individuals should not be left in such environment for more than six days, because after that time the damage done to the psyche cannot be undone.[157]

This is very similar to what the Anne Hamilton-Byrne cult was pretending to do. The therapy consisted of giving a child hallucinogenic doses of LSD, and locking them in a dark room.

There is virtually no publicly available information on the Anne Hamilton-Byrne cult. Whatever exists, has been classified "Top Secret" by the Australian government. It makes one wonder why the they would do that? From what we know, it looks to be a classic CIA operation. The "patients," most of them children, using a deniable cut-out (Anne Hamilton-Byrne cult) were part of a ghastly experiment. Like other CIA guinea pigs under the MK-ULTRA program, they were unwitting and expendable test subjects. Was Assange part of one such experiment? These operations had a fringe benefit: since the tests were taking place outside the United States and on non-US citizens there was another layer of deniability, and responsibility for the outcome of the experiments was further removed.

Another one of CIA's many bags of tricks was a series of experiments with "psychic driving techniques, [where] a patient would be kept in [an] isolated room – the 'sleep room' – and would be administered some combination of drugs and electroconvulsive therapy (electroshock).... This method is, if anything, even more hellish than depatterning, and involves blasting the subject with tape recordings of verbal messages ... that played in a loop for sixteen hours a day for weeks. Normally, two tapes were used: the first was a 'negative conditioning' tape which concentrated on the negative facts of the subject's life, continually reinforcing these unhealthy images. This would then be replaced by a 'positive conditioning' tape, also in a loop, also for sixteen hours a day for weeks."[158]

The end product of such a cult is a group of severely impaired people, one of which might easily be Julian Assange. There is nothing out there that can confirm unequivocally that Assange is a mind control test subject, but as of this writing, there is simply too much circumstantial evidence to discard that possibility.

What he seems to have gotten out of his childhood experience is a tremendous, anti-authoritarian hatred for governments and corporations. How did this deep-rooted mistrust of authority reflect on Assange's personal development? And how can it help us penetrate the depth of his inner self? What clues does it leave behind to the real Assange?

The following email, to an unknown recipient, written by Assange on December 13, 2006, gives us a glimpse into his mindset. Based on new sources that have recently come to light, a new picture of Assange emerges, specifically dealing with his personal and political concerns. On the one hand, in the mainstream interviews he comes out cryptic, dispassionate and faintly self-important. On the other hand, as can be judged from Assange's take on the media circus, he comes across as very media savvy:

From:
Date: Fri, 5 Jan 2007 13:36:51 +1100
To:

We can turn this unexpected difficulty into a great blessing by being crafty and exuberant in our attentions over the next few days.

The hunger for freedom and truth is clearly so intense that despite having little more than "we're working on it" and a nice example (that few seem bother to read in their quest for the salacious) off it goes on its own exponential of media read, write and rewrite. Random quotes (not from us) and rephrasing will lead to the most salacious evolving in the Galapagos of quote, edit and requote.

What this means is that we have to answer questions before they're asked and we have to answer them with statements that optimize max (journalistic lazynes + quote sexyness).

Analogously, the public sphere is warm milk, into which has leaked our culture. Bacterial growth follows an exponential -- left unmolested it would become the congealed yogurt of our desires, but random innocents and malefactors alike are injecting their their own bacterial strain into the mix. The impact of early strains of information release (ours and others) will be fantastically amplified by the exponential process. Consequently we must expend as much energies on this IMMEDIATELY as we have inorder to set path of future perceptions, which will otherwise require far more energies to correct even a day later.

Since we can not seal the public sphere from the influence of others, our only recourse is to continually inject our informational strain into the ferment. If we keep our strain (our public positioning) consistent and quotable we should come to dominate the culture when opposed by relatively random influences of others.

And despite JYAs seasoned fears, our opponents thus far are essentially uncoordinated; they do not strike with vigor at the same point. Here follows our blessing. Because WL has not yet generated ANY specific enemies (at least outside of China and Somalia), attacks are generalized ("pro-censorship") , unmotivated, limp-wristed and lack precision and common direction.

This will not be the case once we release substantial material. That will invoke enemies with specific grievances. Our previous desire to splash forth only with a fully operational system with content would have generated both specific opposition and fears by example.

Hence we have a great opportunity -- to push our desired perceptions of what WL is into the world, to set the key in which future bars of our song are to be played by the public orchestra, BEFORE it faces any serious opposition.[159]

And this:

> Fwd from Julian:

>

> We should be consistent in our use and invention of language. A word or a phrase extracts meaning

> from its resonance with other usages and our experiences. For instance in the FAQ we sometimes use > the phrase "ethical leaking." Should we always use this phrase? 'leak' by itself carries a negative.

> 'ethical' a strong positive. 'ethical leaking' a positive. But it does isolate 'leaks' as being non-ethical

> unless we stick 'ethical' on them. Can we make a movement from this phrase and others? 'The ethical

 > leaking movement'. Powerful. Can it survive the heat of our vision?

Ethical leaking has a nice ring to it, doesn't it? The obvious attack on

 this is that WL cannot distinguish ethical from unethical leaking. However, emphasising that WL seeks to enable ethical leaking is a good idea, it seems to me.

> We must find our own 'Operation Iraqi Freedom' s -- blessings and

 sanctifications that even our most > diseased and demonic opponents will find themselves chanting to each other in the night.

>

> We need a phrases for 'leak facilitator', 'mail drop volunteer', 'ethical leaker', 'wl server operator' etc, etc.

>

> http://www.apache-ssl.org/ben.html http://www.links.org/[160]

There is an understanding in Assange's writing that language, like love and death, alters us and affirms us, clings to us and explores us ("A word or a phrase extracts meaning from its resonance with other usages and our experiences"); that it involves the irrevocable, and makes us who we are.

Although we do not yet see the contours of the media savvy, present day Assange, the next email shows us another facet of him: The romantic dream in that flash of inspiration mingling the ardor of love and the ache of exile. Pay attention to Assange's observational ability, his analytical skills and his very curious reflections on the nature of the Vietnamese psyche. To my mind, something else comes through his reflections. It took me a while to see it: The ominous flaw (the pothole), the banal hollow note, and glib hardly perceivable suggestion that love is doomed, since it can never recapture the miracle of its initial moments.

Wednesday 13, Dec 2006

Dear

How have you been? How's xxxxxx and xxxxxx? [name removed when the correspondence was posted on Cryptome.org] From reading your blog, it seems like the course you are on is sustaining you and people you care about.

Other than to catching up, would you like to join the initial advisory board of an organization that's designing and deploying a censorship resistant version of wikipedia (mediawiki) for mass document leaking? More about that later. I want to give you time to think about what it may mean (technically and politically) in the light of John Young's proven ability to withstand censorship of some very important, but smaller scale leaks on Cryptome.

3 FBI meetings, but no raids. What it doesn't mean is lots of your time. I think even your name would be a positive contribution.

There's a recent picture of me and my daughter (!) on xxxxxxxxxxx, although the rest is mostly decontexualised.

I see you've acquired an interest in motorcycles. Me too.

[I liked the following part of my letter to you so much, I took the non personal bits and published them here xxxxxxxxxxxxxxxxxxx -- please excuse the style change!]

It seems like everyone I meet plans to follow the young Che Guavara, and take off on their motorbike and adventure through the poverty and pleasurs[sic] of South and Central American, now that seduction of random latinos has been politically sanctified -- and who can blame them?

Last year I rode my motorcycle from Ho Chi Min City (Saigon) to Hanoi, up the highway that borders the South China Sea.

The road to Hanoi is a Vietnamese economic artery but is nonetheless dominated by potholes, thousands the size of bomb craters. There are constant reminders of "The American War" all over

Vietnam, and perhaps this was one of them, but in a more indirect way.

To a physicist a pothole has an interesting life. It starts out as a few loose stones. As wheels pass over, these stones grind together and against the under surface. Their edges are rounded off and the depression they are in also becomes rounder by their action. The stones become pestles to the hole's motor. Smaller stones and grit move between the spaces of larger stones and add to the grinding action. The hole enlarges, and deepens. Small stones are soon entirely worn away, but in the process liberate increasingly larger stones from the advancing edge of the hole. The increasing depth and surface capture more and more energy from passing wheels. The destruction of the road surface accelerates until the road is abandoned or the hole is filled.

Road decay is, like a dental decay, a run away process. Utility rapidly diminishes and costs of repair accelerate, and just like teeth it is more efficient to fill a pothole as soon as it is noticed.

But this measure of efficiency is not the metric of politics and it is a political feedback process that lies behind the filling in of potholes on almost every road on earth.

That process is driven by the behavior of politically influential road users who are themselves motivated to action by psychologically negative encounters with potholes.

When potholes are small, the resultant political pressures are not sufficient to overcome the forces of other interests groups who compete for labour and resources. Likewise, it is difficult to motivate people who have other passions and pains in their life to go to the dentist when their teeth do not ache. Both are caused by limitations in knowledge and its distillation: foresight.

Why is this surprising? It is surprising because we are used to looking at government spending through the lens of economic utility; a lens which claims the political process as a derivative. This vision claims that political forces compete for access to the treasury to further their own utility. Hence, military intelligence and public health compete with road maintenance for funding and so should attempt to minimize the latter's drain on the treasury. But that drain is minimized by filling in potholes immediately!

Foresight requires trustworthy information about the current state of the world, cognitive ability to draw predictive inferences and economic stability to give them a meaningful home. It's not only in Vietnam where secrecy, malfeasance and unequal access have eaten into the first requirement of foresight ("truth and lots of it").

Foresight can produce outcomes that leave all major interests groups better off. Likewise the lack of it, or doing the dumb thing, can harm almost everyone.

Computer scientists have long had a great phrase for the dependency of foresight on trustworthy information; "garbage in, garbage out."

In intelligence agency oversight we have "The Black Budget blues," but the phrase is probably most familiar to us as "The Fox News Effect" of the world, cognitive ability to draw predictive inferences and economic stability to give them a meaningful home. It's not only in Vietnam where secrecy, malfeasance and unequal access have eaten into the first requirement of foresight ("truth and lots of it").

But back in the west and a land of cars, I noted that I knew only 10 people who had died; two murders, one suicide and six dead or severely brain damaged in motorcycle accidents. None from old age, which reflects my clans' longevity and wanderlust on one hand and fractiousness on the other. I stopped riding in the land of cars.

Cheers,[161]

The underlying thought is the impotence of man in the path of all-devouring, indifferent nature – the cosmic will of Schoepenhauer. Life is a temporary consolation. Life cannot resist the ineluctable, blind march of nature, which knows neither art nor freedom nor the good. Nature creates, even as she destroys – she is concerned only that life should go on, and that death should not lose its right.

*****

Lights. Camera. Action. A different Assange emerges into the spotlight. A chameleon. An opportunist. A zealot. Someone elusive, evasive, someone duplicitous. He speaks of the dark forces at work. Are these the same "dark forces" Allen Dulles referred to in his 1953 Princeton University, in which he characterized the Cold War as a Manichean struggle between the forces of Light and Darkness? One of the trademarks of a mind control victim is the similarity in their vocabulary, when describing certain events. Memories and suggestions are implanted without the victim's knowledge. The mind becomes a blank slate, on which one redraws the most sinister convictions of Evil.

In a July 18, 2010 article/interview with *The Independent*'s Matthew Bell, where Assange told "why governments fear WikiLeaks[162]," Bell commented:

> Spending time with Assange, it's hard not to start believing that dark forces are at work. According to him, everyone's emails are being read. For that reason, he encourages anyone planning to leak a document to post it the old fashioned way, to his PO Box.[163]

Ronald Thomas West, a former sergeant of Operations and Intelligence for Special Forces makes a very interesting point when he states:

> NO-no-no Julian Assange, it does not work like that unless you wish to do intelligence agencies like the CIA a big favor — the daily 1.6 billion "everyones" email collected by American intelligence cannot be read, it is a logistical impossibility. Text extraction computing software is imperfect and pick ups by far more false leads than real leads and 'read mails' of those people singled out for surveilliance [sic] (like myself) can read by more than one country's agencies, including law enforcement (a fact for which I am personally pleased) and that is how, among other things, Italian law enforcement can bring down a criminal CIA rendition"It is actually much easier for intelligence agencies to track the physical mail system. It leaves tangible clues: postmarks, finger prints, DNA... whereas the experienced someone who is keen not to be monitored or discovered while whistle-blowing crimes (unlike myself, I do not need to conceal my identity) working inside/outside the system will leak with a untraceable to the source used or stolen laptop at a wire-

less café where one can create an online email account in minutes, attach, upload and send documents in a few minutes more, abandon the mail account, wipe the drive, destroy and dispose of [dumpster] the computer and never frequent that particular wireless café again. Another means is upload from a parked car sitting in the street, having found a random open wireless signal and DO NOT leak to WikiLeaks.

Trained intelligence people know this. Trained counter intelligence people would also want Julian Assange putting out the word to use physical a P.O. Box to leak, so they can better track leaks to their source. Assange profiles for CIA....

"Because in 'intelligence,' particularly when it comes to counter-intelligence and psy-ops (psychological operations) truth is a relative thing and the problem with that is, truth being relative is not healthy. It is not healthy for people and it is not healthy for society."[164]

LINKS TO THE INTELLIGENCE COMMUNITY

As I stated in my 2005 Bilderberg report, "If democracy is the rule of the people, secret government agendas and influence-peddling sinister cliques are incompatible with democracy. The people cannot possibly rule on something they don't know about. The whole idea of clandestine spheres of influence within the government waging secret campaigns is therefore foreign to the notion of democracy and must be fought with zealous determination lest we wish to repeat the fatal errors of the not-so-distant past."[165]

Shrouded in secrecy, "WikiLeaks feels the need to reassure public opinion that it has no contacts with the intelligence community. Ironically, it also sees the need to define the activities of the intelligence agencies and compare them to those of WikiLeaks."[166] Let's listen to what they have to say:

1.5 The people behind WikiLeaks

WikiLeaks is a project of the Sunshine Press. It's probably pretty clear by now that WikiLeaks is not a front for any intelligence agency or government despite a rumour to that effect. This rumour was started early in WikiLeaks' existence, possibly by the intelligence agencies themselves. WikiLeaks is an independent global group of people with a long standing dedication to the idea of a free press and the improved transparency in society that comes from this. The group includes accredited journalists, software programmers, network engineers, mathematicians and others.

To determine the truth of our statements on this, simply look at the evidence. By definition, intelligence agencies want to hoard information. By contrast, WikiLeaks has shown that it wants to do just the opposite. Our track record shows we go to great lengths to bring the truth to the world without fear or favour.[167]

Assange has implied that rumors about any intelligence agency links should be read as none other than a sign of WikiLeaks "success." That any campaign for the truth is but a sign of their desperation." "Newspeak and doublethink, the totalitarian 'reality control' devices that Orwell described so thoroughly in *1984*, don't always take the form of the simple messages that are common to it."[168] We've heard this kind of reasoning before. War Is Peace, Hate Is Love, Slavery Is Freedom. *Arbeit Macht Frei*.

Beware of false prophets.

Its underlying principles, after all, are the interposition of two seemingly contradictory ideas or concepts and asserting that they are identical, thereby nullifying their meanings. This concept can apply to whole reconstructions of reality – particularly in the rewriting of history that contravenes reality and substantive fact, asserting the opposite of that reality to be true, and offering distorted or utterly false evidence in support and asserting that it is true. The most notorious manifestation of violence is Holocaust denial and similar forms of historical revisionism.[169]

"Is WikiLeaks a CIA front?" asks Assange in a rhetorical question for the audience's benefit. And the reply:

> WikiLeaks is not a front for the CIA, MI6, FSB or any other agency. Quite the opposite actually. [...] By definition spy agencies want to hide information. We want to get it out to the public.[170]

"Quite true. But by definition, a covert operation always pretends to be something it is not, and never claims to be what it is."[171] In other words, it can't be identified as an official CIA project, so it must seem to be the opposite of what it is. For any false flag operation to be effective, 90% of what you put out has to be legitimate information; only then will you be able to target the people with disinformation for completely different reasons.

So, how is this all linked to the real world?

In her globalresearch.ca December 20, 2010 article, Julie Lévesque quotes Daniel Tencer in explaining the role played by some of the leading members of the Obama administration, especially Cass Sunstein, who heads the Obama White House's Office of Information and Regulatory Affairs. Sunstein is also the author of a Harvard Law School essay entitled "Conspiracy Theories: Causes and Cures."

> [Sunstein] argued that the government should stealthily infiltrate groups that pose alternative theories on historical events via 'chat rooms, online social networks, or even real-space groups and attempt to undermine' those groups....
>
> Sunstein means that people who believe in conspiracy theories have a limited number of sources of information that they trust. Therefore, Sunstein argued in the article, it would not work to simply refute the conspiracy theories in public — the very sources that conspiracy theorists believe would have to be infiltrated.
>
> Sunstein, whose article focuses largely on the 9/11 conspiracy theories, suggests that the government "enlist

non-governmental officials in the effort to rebut the theories. It might ensure that credible independent experts offer the rebuttal, rather than government officials themselves. There is a tradeoff between credibility and control, however. The price of credibility is that government cannot be seen to control the independent experts.[172]

In other words, Sunstein says, let's pose as patriots online. Let's disrupt the 9/11 Truth movement. Let's put out our own disinformation. "The purpose is not to suppress dissent, but, on the contrary, to shape and mould the protest movement, to set the outer limits of dissent." How? Through regulating, monitoring, limiting and controlling the opposition. "What must be protected and sustained are the interests of the economic elites, which control the political apparatus from behind the scenes."[173]

What does Assange do? He openly attacks the same people his alternative, independent, anti-authoritarian movement should be defending. This is a classic tactic of intelligence operations. Infiltrate, divide and conquer. Regulate, limit and control.

Are we to believe that WikiLeaks is indeed dedicated to the principle that "seeking change, does not mean seeking or resorting to violence, but proactive effort to bring about positive change at all levels, individual and collective?"[175] The old adage that the reason for war is to end war can't be considered wise, especially when war has become the means to incite armed conflict that far surpasses the original reason for the violent struggle.

> Since each of us is enclosed forever in a consciousness to which no one else can ever have access, democracy is the natural condition of every man ever since the human mind became conscious not only of the world but of itself.[176]

We must not turn our backs on inhumanity and violence. We must separate the phony from the serious, the authentic from the counterfeit. In other words, we must act with wisdom. Assange speaks of "courage and strength" when dealing with "authoritarian power structures" and of duty to "expose oppressing or major crimes." Is that him posing as patriot? Certainly, there are deep-rooted misgivings about Assange's real take on the most pressing issues of our time.

ASSANGE AND SEPTEMBER 11, 2001

Economist F. William Engdahl makes a compelling case in questioning Assange's true intentions: "A closer examination of the public position of Assange on one of the most controversial issues of recent decades, the forces behind the September 11, 2001 attacks on the Pentagon and World Trade Center shows him to be curiously establishment. When the *Belfast Telegraph* interviewed him on July 19, he stated, 'Any time people with power plan in secret, they are conducting a conspiracy. So there are conspiracies everywhere. There are also crazed conspiracy theories. It's important not to confuse these two....' *What about 9/11?*: 'I'm constantly annoyed that people are distracted by false conspiracies such as 9/11, when all around we provide evidence of real conspiracies, for war or mass financial fraud.' *What about the Bilderberg Conference?*: 'That is vaguely conspiratorial, in a networking sense. We have published their meeting notes.'"[177]

Think about it. If you are coming out with revelations that the government does not want you to know, such as what really happened on 9/11, you don't get the *New York Times*, the *Guardian* and *Der Spiegel* cooperating with you. *Der Spiegel* had a major cover story on conspiracy fanatics who turn the world upside down. The German magazine openly stated that serious investigators who are following up on 9/11 are lunatics and anti-Semites. *Der Spiegel*'s position seem to coincide with Assange's position in that both of them are irritated by people investigating the greatest crime of the 21st century – September 11, 2001. Both *Der Spiegel* and Assange refer to the people involved as "crazy conspiracy theorists."[178]

Engdahl continues:

> That statement from a person who has built a reputation of being anti-establishment is more than notable. First, as thousands of physicists, engineers, military professionals and airline pilots have testified, the idea that 19 barely-trained Arabs armed with box-cutters could divert four US commercial jets and execute the near-impossible strikes on the Twin Towers and Pentagon over a time period of 93 minutes with not one Air Force NORAD military interception, is beyond belief. Precisely who executed the professional attack is a matter for genuine unbiased international inquiry.
>
> Notable for Mr. Assange's blunt denial of any sinister 9/11 conspiracy is the statement in a BBC interview by former US Senator, Bob Graham, who chaired the United States Senate Select Committee on Intelligence when it performed its Joint Inquiry into 9/11. Graham told BBC, 'I can just state that within 9/11 there are too many secrets, that is information that has not been made available to the public for which there are specific tangible credible answers and that the withholding of those secrets has eroded public confidence in their government as it relates to their own security.' BBC narrator: 'Senator Graham found that the cover-up led to the heart of the administration.' Bob Graham: 'I called the White House and talked with Ms. Rice and said, 'Look, we've been told we're gonna get cooperation in this inquiry, and she said she'd look into it, and nothing happened.'
>
> Of course, the Bush Administration was able to use the 9/11 attacks to launch its War on Terrorism in Afghanistan and then Iraq, a point Assange conveniently omits.[179]

Again, a man orchestrating this online government effort to discredit the 9/11 Truth movement is one of President Obama's closest collaborators, Cass Sunstein.

WHO IS CASS SUNSTEIN?

Longtime Obama friend, Sunstein, is an animal-rights cultist, who is married to National Security Council official Samantha Power. According to Tony Papert, in *Executive Intelligence Review* "He declares that animals have human-like rights and should be able to bring suit in court, through human lawyers, against violations of these rights. Animal rights? That's really just the flip side of believing that humans are animals—animals who should be enslaved because they are irrational and therefore must be controlled. This is the bestiality and degeneracy of the British Empire being openly displayed by the Obama government aparatchiks. Picture lines of pigs wearing swastika brossards on their arms."[180]

Papert goes on, "According to a *Time* [April 13, 2009] account, ... the President has been surrounded by a collection of 'behaviorist economists,' who have cultivated a cult-like following through the publication of such daffy economic tracts as *Freakonomics*, *Nudge*, *Predictable Irrationality*, *The Wisdom of Crowds*, and *Animal Spirits*. These economists, including long-time Obama advisor Cass Sunstein ... have formed a tight clique ... of the Pavlovian/Skinnerian kooks...."[181]

In fact, the crazies working within the confines of Obama's White House "are not really economists at all, but psychological warfare specialists disguising their psywar measures as economic policy. They are all hard-core followers of the British philosophical radicalism of John Locke, Bernard de Mandeville, Adam Smith, and Jeremy Bentham, the 18th-Century creatures who argued that man is nothing more than a beast, irrationally driven by pleasure and pain."[182] No wonder Cass Sunstein fits so snugly into this group.

> Though couched in pseudo-scientific terms, and presented as New Age self-help and personal empowerment measures, the policies these behaviorists are pushing are designed to dehumanize the population, to turn us into

even more of a herd of frightened sheep than we are already. Now that the financial bubble has popped, they say, it is time for a new paradigm, one which will prepare us for the coming collapse of living standards, and of population levels. These policies will be presented as positive—stopping "global warming," learning to live simpler lives, doing with less as a way of saving the planet. Underneath this feel-good pop psychology is pure fascism.[183]

With the bursting of the economic bubble, the economic behaviorism also needed to change, "requiring an alteration of the brainwashing programming. Whereas the old-style 'neo-classical economics,' with its assertion that man acted in his 'rational self-interest,' was useful in convincing the people that the 'markets' knew what they were doing, and that the bubble was good for the nation and good for the people, that era has passed."[184] That's where WikiLeaks would come in as the agent of change and propaganda.

Now the people are to be told something else: that the bubble was wrong, that we went too far, that we are killing the planet, and that changes, and sacrifices, must be made. We must be "green," we must not only accept, but desire, a lower standard of living. We are, in effect, being prepared to pay the bill for the bailout, and for the destruction it will produce." In other words "preparing the people for the pain is where the 'behavioral economists' come in.[185]

And if WikiLeaks is a long-range by-product of the unseen policy planners, then promoting the green agenda is most certainly in their interests. How many hundreds of thousands of documents will it take to convince the world that progress is wrong?

Environmentalist movement=Green=deindustrialization =zero growth=population reduction=genocide

In fact, citing a *New Federalist* newspaper slide presentation, "the post-World War II environmental movement, was nothing but a revival of the Eugenics Movement of the late nineteenth and early 20th century. After the Nazi genocide, the term "eugenics" was discredited, so the same British and allied European and North American elites who backed Hitler changed the name to environmentalism and went right back into the genocide business. To illustrate the point: WWF founder Sir Julian Huxley was president of the Eugenics Society in 1961 when the WWF came into being."[186]

Helga Zepp-Larouche makes it interesting when she refers to technological progress as the base of all evil for the Green Party. "In case someone requires proof that the Greens march in fascist footsteps, then one should refer to the modern identity of the argumentation of Friedrich Georg Junger in *The Perfection of Technology*, written in 1939....

> He [Junger] warns of the dangerous illusions that are associated with technological progress.... Technology fills the air with smoke, pollutes the water, destroys forests and animals. This leads to a condition, in which Nature must be protected from rational thought." Does that sound familiar? It should. Under the guise of global warming, we are being bombarded with this message almost daily by the mainstream press across the world. Then Junger states the following, "The technician ruins factory owners through inventions which are not anticipated. The wealth and ruin of the capitalists is as indifferent to him as that of the proletariat."[187]

And then, the magic word, the key idea is stated: "Technological progress ruins interest!"[188]

In reality, by cutting down productivity, through cutting down infrastructure, by cutting inventions, technology, you are forcing a collapse in population. The plan of the moneyed elite has always been to destroy the human mind because, as I explained in my European Parliament presentation on the Bilderberg group, "Human mind affects the development of the Planet. This is how mankind is measured. What separates us from animals is our ability to discover universal physical principles. It allows us to innovate, which subsequently improves the lives of people."[189]

On the other hand, the Empire of money depends upon suppression of scientific development and knowledge by keeping us backwards and dumb. And if you keep people stupid and not too numerous, then the minority can control them. According to Bilderberg, there is no such thing as a scientific principle. The problem here is the conception of what truth is: In the Bilderberg-led system, the truth doesn't exist. Because it is an imperialist system. No truth. Only the arrogance of power.

This arrogance of power can be summed up through another one of the elite's key initiatives in that "technology is responsible for inflation."[190] The IMF uses the same propaganda, "solely for the purpose of keeping developing nations, which want to progress with their industrialisation, under the yoke of colonialism."[191]

The theses proposed by Junger at the beginning are emphasised in the following way: "We must recognise that technological progress and the education of the masses go hand in hand." Some twenty years later, Bertrand Russell picked up on the theme of education and expanded it even further. "It [education] will be rigidly confined to the governing class...When the technique has been perfected, every government that has been in charge of education will be able to control its subjects without the need of armies or policeman."[192] In other words, "for the oligarchy, educated masses – numerous educated people – is a horrible idea, because they would end their privileged, elitist position as oligarchs, who are happy to rule over uneducated masses."[193]

And that's where Cass Sunstein, the animal rights cultist, anti-humanist degenerate and behavioral economist fits so snugly.

John Hoefle in the April 17, 2009 edition of EIR explains:

> These policies are particularly aimed at the children and grandchildren of the Baby Boomers, the generations

which have rejected the "reality" of the Boomers in favour of creating one of their own. These youth have seen what a mess their parents and grandparents made of the world and want no part of it, but they have no real sense of identity around which to properly diagnose and remedy the disaster they are inheriting. As a result, they've largely opted out, indifferent to the world in which they live, preferring to escape into entertainment, amusements, and narcissism.[194]

Looks and smells very much like Assange, a man with no real sense of identity and no theoretical basis to any of his positions. He is certainly not anti-war. He does not say that the US should get out of Afghanistan and stop interfering in Pakistan. What Assange is saying is: "whatever you want to do, be transparent and be humane." He does not talk about imperialism. He does not talk about Anglo-American banking, New World Order; he does not talk about any concept that may allow someone to make sense of his political beliefs. There is no element of that at all. Instead, we are subjected to a series of cute sound bites. Nothing profound, just fuzzy and warm feel-good platitudes.

Like this one, for example, taken from his Assange email on January 5, 2007:

> Principled leaking has changed the course of history for the better; it can alter the course of history in the present; it can lead us to a better future.[195]

What does it mean? Does Assange know?

If you are wondering why I am asking this, the reason is quite simple. "Most people don't know where their opinions come from.... Much of what is generally considered personal opinion is actually the result of decades of brainwashing delivered through our educational system, our entertainment and news media, the ever-present advertising, and more recently, the Internet."[196] And that's another facet of the WikiLeaks operation we should consider.

We get a glimpse of that in Assange's interview with *Time*, in which he explained that secretive organizations need to be exposed:

If their behavior is revealed to the public, they have one of two choices: one is to reform in such a way that they can be proud of their endeavors, and proud to display them to the public. Or the other is to lock down internally and to balkanize, and as a result, of course, cease to be as efficient as they were. To me, that is a very good outcome, because organizations can either be efficient, open and honest, or they can be closed, conspiratorial and inefficient.[197]

Assange further explained some of his perspectives regarding the influence of and reactions to WikiLeaks, stating that the Chinese:

... appear to be terrified of free speech, and while one might say that means something awful is happening in the country, I actually think that is a very optimistic sign, because it means that speech can still cause reform and that the power structure is still inherently political, as opposed to fiscal. So journalism and writing are capable of achieving change, and that is why Chinese authorities are so scared of it. Whereas in the United States to a large degree, and in other Western countries, the basic elements of society have been so heavily fiscalized through contractual obligations that political change doesn't seem to result in economic change, which in other words means that political change doesn't result in change.[198]

So, according to Julian Assange, journalism and writing are capable of achieving change in China, but not in the Western world and certainly not in the United States. Is that because the corporate media is owned by special interests interlocked with powerful forces above government level, such as the Bilderberg group, Trilateral Commission, Council on Foreign Relations, etc? How would the government remedy this perception of reality? Obviously, by creating a parallel reality with the help of psychological warfare specialists such as Cass Sunstein and company.

BEHAVIORAL ECONOMIST ROUNDTABLE

"The core of this group of behaviorist kooks is the Behavioral Economist Roundtable,"[199] "a secret advisory group of 29 of the nation's leading behaviorists." Not exactly. The group of 29 is actually called the Behavioral Economics Roundtable, based in the Russell Sage Foundation in Washington, D.C. It is a self-selecting, self-perpetuating group, just like Cecil Rhodes' Round Table which governed the British Empire for the Fabian Society."[200] "These foundations are offshoots of the same treasonous, pro-British networks who supported Hitler and Mussolini, created the fascist American Liberty League, and fought President Franklin Roosevelt at every turn. They were fascist then, and they are fascist now."[201]

Few people realise that a clique of "behavioral economists" controls billions of dollars in private assets, mostly through illicit criminal activity.

"An institutional base for the 'behavioral economists' is the National Bureau of Economic Research (NBER), a think tank located next door to Harvard University in Cambridge, Massachusetts. NBER states that its "workshop in behavioral economics" has been sponsored since 2001 by three private firms: 'Bracebridge Capital, Fuller & Thaler Asset Management, and LSV Asset Management.'

> The smallest of the three interlocking funds, with about $1 billion in assets, is Fuller & Thaler. Its boss Richard Thaler founded and has directed the NBER program since 1991. Thaler helps coordinate the Summers gang's policy control through Thaler's close associates Austan Goolsbee (Obama Presidential campaign chief economist), and Cass Sunstein (Federal Regulatory Czar)....
> The next largest fund sponsoring the NBER program is Bracebridge Capital, with over $3 billion and possibly

double that in assets under management. It is owned by Nancy Zimmerman and her husband Andrei Shleifer.

Harvard Professor Shleifer is Lawrence Summers' protege and personal international agent. Shleifer's own fortune is estimated in the hundred of millions, perhaps a billion dollars. This wealth was generated in the 1990s Summers/Shleifer/Harvard scandal in Russia. Summers, then a World Bank official, had sent Shleifer to Russia to run a U.S.-funded program to privatize Soviet assets into private hands. The program collapsed when Shleifer was caught diverting and hiding the assets for himself, using his wife's firm.

The Shleifer family firm now known as Bracebridge paid $1.5 million in 2004, to settle a U.S. government suit charging that Shleifer and his wife's firm had improperly used USAID-funded resources and staff and ... diverted US taxpayer resources for its own purposes and profit....

The largest private fund sponsoring the NBER program is LSV Asset Management, in control of $35 billion.... Around 2005 or 2006, sometime before the global offshore finance bubble blew out, Andrei Shleifer sold his share of LVS, [which stands for its founders, Lakonishok, Shleifer and Vishny], netting him perhaps around $400 million.[202]

The Battle for 'Transparency'

"Assange encourages blind faith in WikiLeaks as he puts a lot of emphasis on the trustworthiness of his opaque organization."[203] But the attack on 9/11 Truth is most significant. What he is really saying is, "the conspiracy theories that are approved are my conspiracy theories, and the rest of the theories are the domain of the lunatic fringe."

In the words of Assange:

Once something starts going around and being considered trustworthy in a particular arena, and you meet someone and they say 'I heard this is trustworthy,' then all of a sudden it reconfirms your suspicion that the thing is trustworthy. So that's why brand is so important, just as it is with anything you have to trust."[204]

People should understand that WikiLeaks has proven to be arguably the most trustworthy new source that exists, because we publish primary source material and analysis based on that primary source material," Assange told CNN. "Other organizations, with some exceptions, simply are not trustworthy.[205]

Investigative journalist Julie Lévesque gets to the point in her globalresearch, December 20, 2010 article:

> While WikiLeaks no longer discloses the names of the members of its advisory board, nor does it reveal its sources of funding, we have to trust it because according to its founder Julian Assange, it has proven to be the most trustworthy news source that exists.
>
> Moreover, if we follow Assange's assertion that there are only a few media organizations which can be considered trustworthy, we must assume that those are the ones which were selected by WikiLeaks to act as 'partners' in the release and editing of the leaks, including The New York Times, Der Spiegel The Guardian, El Païs, [and] Le Monde.
>
> Yet The New York Times, which employs members of the Council on Foreign Relations (CFR) including WikiLeaks' collaborator David E. Sanger, has proven more than once to be a propaganda tool for the US government, the most infamous example being the Iraqi WMD narrative promoted by Pulitzer Prize winner Judith Miller." Would Assange be aware of this?" Of course he would. It is his organization in the first place, responsible for leaking the allegedly secret documents.
>
> In an interview, Assange indicates that WikiLeaks chose a variety of media to avoid the use of leaks for propaganda purposes. It is important to note that although these media might be owned by different groups and have different editorial policies, they are without exception news entities controlled by major Western media corporations.

A much better way to avoid the use of leaks for disinformation purposes would have been to work with media from different regions of the world (e.g. Asia, Latin America, Middle East) as well as establish partnership agreements with the alternative media. By working primarily with media organizations from NATO countries [and belonging to Bilderberg's inner circle], WikiLeaks has chosen to submit its leaks to one single 'worldview', that of the West.[206]

The view of One World Company Ltd.

WikiLeaks' Entourage.
Who Supports WikiLeaks?

John Young is a 74-year old architect from New York who publishes a document-leaking Web site called Cryptome. org that predates WikiLeaks by over a decade. He quit WikiLeaks, claiming the operation was a CIA front. His parting words: "WikiLeaks is a fraud... working for the enemy."

On October 3, 2006, Young was approached by the WikiLeaks founders, and asked to hold the Wikileaks.org domain registration. On Dec 8, 2006, John was added to the WikiLeaks e-mail list.

According to Lévesque "Young became very skeptical concerning the WikiLeaks project specifically with regard to the initial fund-raising goal of 5 million dollars, the contacts with elite organizations including Freedom House and the National Endowment for Democracy mentioned earlier"[207] and the alleged millions of documents:

> [Young] "Announcing a $5 million fund-raising goal by July will kill this effort. It makes WL appear to be a Wall Street scam. This amount could not be needed so soon except for suspect purposes. I'd say the same about the alleged 1.1 million documents ready for leaking. Way too many to be believable without evidence. I don't be-

lieve the number. So far, one document, of highly suspect provenance."

Instead, explain what funding needs there are and present a schedule for their need, avoid generalities and lump sums. Explain how the funds will be managed and protected against fraud and theft....

BTW, the biggest crooks brag overmuch of how ethical their operations are. Avoid ethical promises, period, they've been used too often to fleece victims. Demonstrate sustained ethical behavior, don't preach/peddle it.

The CIA would be the most likely $5M funder. Soros is suspected of being a conduit for black money to dissident groups racketeering for such payola.

Now it may be that that is the intention of WL because its behavior so far fits the pattern."

Assange responds:

Advice noted. We'll polish up our sheers for cutting fleeces golden.

It is hard to tell whether Assange's comment was meant to be serious, but Young went berserk:

"Fuck your cute hustle and disinformation campaign against legitimate dissent. Same old shit, working for the enemy...WikiLeaks is a fraud," he announced. "Cryptome is publishing the contents of this list, and how I was induced to serve as US person for registration."[208]

Young clarified his view on WikiLeaks in a written exchange with Evan James, fact-checker at *Mother Jones* magazine. "WikiLeaks set out to raise $5 million as soon as possible. That's what remains its primary mission, as recently demonstrated and thus totally untrustworthy for information but fabulous entertainment in the leakage vein."[209]

On December 7, 2010, Young, in a scathing critique of the site, confirmed his earlier point: "WikiLeaks are for-hire mercenaries...WikiLeaks has always been a commercial enterprise hiding behind a narcissistic 'public interest' PR."[210]

Information published on Young's cryptome.org from someone claiming to be a 'WikiLeaks insider' is quite telling in this respect. "Since January 2010 WikiLeaks income until end of April 2010 has been:

Internet Donations: $132,347 USD
Paid Media Interviews and Appearances etc. $82,892 USD
Sponsorships: $28,657 USD

The total income YTD is $243,896 USD."[211]

This individual further claims that "the lack of any significant high rollers backing Assange has led to a significant change of direction concerning fund raising. Keeping in mind that Assange has publicly stated that he needs $200,000 USD just to keep the lights on, and $600,000 USD to be fully funded; then just how much has Assange received, how much has been spent, and on what? A pressing point when one considers WikiLeaks is still effectively closed down, and Assange, up until November 2010, continued to enjoy a particularly luxurious lifestyle, with no comparable income streams."[212]

And, Young has gone even further. "[He] believes WikiLeaks is selling its secrets for commercial gain. Speaking to US talk radio, Young compared Julian Assange to Henry Kissinger, and other 'spook insiders' who have turned their insider knowledge into a lucrative sideline. 'What has been released has been much less voluminous than the attention about them,' said Young. 'The goal is to exaggerate the importance of WikiLeaks'. From the earliest discussions, Young alleges, WikiLeaks intended to pimp out the information for funds.

"Well, it only came up in the topic of raising $5 million the first year. That was the first red flag that I heard about. I thought that they were actually a public interest group up until then, but as soon as I heard that, I knew that they were a criminal organization."[213]

And what of *New York Times'* criticism of WikiLeaks and Assange?,

> The original intention of WikiLeaks, see the emails, was to become wealthy doing what spies do using the two-pronged practice of public service by secret means, ancient and corrupt. Negative criticism of this is water off the duck's back. It is an obligation of spies and the wealthy to attack their kind, pretending opposition to cloak hand in hand.[214]

"Assange is a narcissistic individual," claims Young. In a posting to the nettime mailing list, Young added:

> The free stuff is meant [to] lure volunteers and promote high-profile public service, lipsticked with risk, with the enterprise funded by selling costly material sold on the black market of worldwide spying in the tradition of public benefit ops, ID, spies and ever more spies. No better customers for illicit information that [sic] those with depthless pockets.[215]

Who is behind all this stolen info?

> There is a very large underground economy in stolen information. Some of it comes in using the Internet, other information comes from enlisted man in key positions, still other information comes directly from the government through agencies set up for this purpose and WikiLeaks is a part of that. It is a very small part, but the technology for selling stolen information is very large and very lucrative. Governments do it, operations do it and individuals do it. They basically sell stolen information. But, in order to sell it to the highest bidder, first you have to overvalue it, in order to get the highest price. So, WikiLeaks is engaged in a campaign to raise the price of their information.[216]

In other words, "Assange has not abandoned the concept of selling information by auction to media groups on an exclusive basis. Now just where does that fit into WIKILEAKS philosophy? To put it brutally, it does not, it's a scheme designed exclusively to fill Assange offshore bank accounts."[217] The following posting on Cryptome's server seem to confirm Young's well founded suspicions:

To: John Young <jya[a t]pipeline.com>
From: WikiLeaks <wikileaks[a t]wikileaks.org>
Subject: martha stuart pgp
Date: Sun, 7 Jan 2007 12:20:25 -0500

-----BEGIN PGP MESSAGE-----

Version: None

J. We are going to fuck them all. Chinese mostly, but not entirely a feint. Invention abounds. Lies, twists and distorts everywhere needed for protection. Hackers monitor Chinese and other intel as they burrow into their targets, when they pull, so do we. Inexhaustible supply of material. Near 100,000 documents/ emails a day. We're going to crack the world open and let it flower into something new. If fleecing the CIA will assist us, then fleece we will. We have pullbacks from NED, CFR, Freedom House and other CIA teats. We have all of pre 2005 Afghanistan. Almost all of india fed. Half a dozen foreign ministries. Dozens of political parties and consulates, worldbank, apec, UN sections, trade groups, tibet and fulan dafa associations and... russian phishing mafia who pull data everywhere. We're drowing. We don't even know a tenth of what we have or who it belongs to. We stopped storing it at 1Tb.[218]

In posting to the nettime mailing list, Young added:

Soros and the Kochs have their lesser-known Internet promoters backing WikiLeaks generously. And they expect good return on their investment, not just the freebies used to attract attention.'

Writing last December, Young shared his disgust at WikiLeaks' similar tactics to advertising-supported or state-supported media – which Young claims cannot be trusted by definition.

"WikiLeaks lies as much as the media, indeed, exactly in the advertising format of the media. Its consumers like it for that very reason. It rides the wave of imaginary disgust with MSM and governments, but it has not modified the formula of braggardy and drama essential to capture eyeballs and through eyeballs, minds and hearts."[219]

Indeed a far cry from Wiki's humble beginnings... As leaked through Cryptome.org:

Date: Fri, 29 Dec 2006 06:01:09 +1100
From:
To:

[This is a restricted internal development mailinglist for w-i-k-i-l-e-a-k-s-.-o-r-g.bPlease do not mention that word directly in these discussions; refer instead to 'WL'. This list is housed at riseup.net, an activist collective in Seattle with an established lawyer and plenty of backbone.]

Hi xxxxxxxxx,

Thanks for your kind words.

We've thought long and hard about this.

It's easy to perceive the connection between publication and the complaints people make about publication. But this generates a perception bias, because it overlooks the vastness of the invisible. It overlooks the unintended consequences of failing to publish and it overlooks all those who are emancipated by being in a climate where bad governance cannot be concealed. Such a climate is a motivating force to behave better in the first place and shifts structures and individuals that generate bad governance away from positions where they generate poor governance.

Injustice concealed cannot be answered. Concealed plans for future injustice cannot be stopped until they are revealed by becoming reality, which is too late. Administrative injustice, by definition affects many.

Government has ample avenues to abuse revelation, not limited to the full force of intelligence, law enforcement, and complicit media. Moves towards the democratisation of revelation are strongly biased in favor of justice. Where democratised revelations are unjust they tend to affect isolated individuals, but where they are just, they affect systems of policy, planning an governance and through them the lives of all.

You may point to a salicious main stream media, but that is not democratised revelation. We point instead to the internet as a whole, which although not yet a vehicle of universal free revelation, is very close to it. Look at the great bounty of positive political change pooring forth as a result.

WikiLeaks reveals, but it is not primarily a tool of revelation. There are many avenues on the internet for revelation. What does not exist is a social movement to that makes acting ethically by leaking a virtue. What does not exist is a comfortable way for everyone to leak safely and easily. What does not exist is a way to turn raw leaks into politically influential knowledge through the revolutionary mass collaborative analysis of wikipedia.

Sufficient leaking will bring down many administrations that rely on concealing reality -- including the US administration. Ellsberg calls for it. Everyone knows it. We're doing it.

In relation to timing; We intend to go live with a reduced system in the next month. Until then we are publishing selected analysis inconvential venues to get some material out and encourage assistance. We're gradually scaling up. At the moment we have certain asymmetries- e.g more leaks than we can store or index. It's just a matter of gradually inspiring increasing commitment and resources from generous people. Like yourself :)[220]

Or this from early January 2007:

From:
To:
Date: Fri, 05 Jan 2007 00:36:01 -0600

... The power of principled leaking to embarrass governments, corporations and institutions is amply demonstrated through recent history. Public scrutiny of otherwise unaccountable and secretive institutions pressures them to act ethically. What official will chance a secret, corrupt transaction when the public is likely to find out? What repressive plan will be carried out when it is revealed to the citizenry? When the risks of embarrassment through openness and honesty increase, the tables are turned against conspiracy, corruption, exploitation and oppression. Open government answers injustice rather than causing it. Open government exposes and undoes corruption. Open governance is the most cost effective method of promoting good governance.

Today, with authoritarian governments in power around much of the world, increasing authoritarian tendencies in democratic governments, and increasing amounts of power vested in unaccountable corporations, the need for openness and democratization is greater than ever.

WL is a tool to satisfy that need. WL is cutting out the middleman, reducing the risk to potential leakers, and improving analysis and dissemination of leaked documents. WL provides simple and straightforward means for anonymous and untraceable leaking of documents.

At the same time, WL opens leaked documents up to a much more exacting scrutiny than any media organization or intelligence agency could provide: the scrutiny of a worldwide community of informed wiki editors.

Instead of a couple of academic specialists, WL will provide a forum for the entire global community to examine any document relentlessly for credibility, plausibility, veracity and falsifiability. They will be able to interpret documents and explain their relevance to the public. If a document is leaked from the Chinese government, the entire Chinese dissident community can freely scrutinize and discuss it; if a document is leaked from Somalia, the entire Somali refugee community can analyze it and put it in context. And so on.

WL may become the most powerful intelligence agency on earth, an intelligence agency of the people. It will be an open source, democratic intelligence agency. But it will be far better, far more principled, and far less parochial than any governmental intelligence agency; consequently, it will be more accurate, and more relevant. It will have no commercial or national interests at heart; its only interests will be truth and freedom of information. Unlike the covert activities of national intelligence agencies, WL will rely upon the power of overt fact to inform citizens about the truths of their world.

WL will resonate not to the sound of money or guns or the flow of oil, but to the grievances of oppressed and exploited people around the world. It will be the outlet for every government official, every bureaucrat, every corporate worker, who becomes privy to embarrassing information which the institution wants to hide but the public needs to know. What conscience cannot contain, and institutional secrecy unjustly conceals, WL can broadcast to the world.

WL will be a forum for the ethical defection of unaccountable and abusive power to the people. WL will be an anvil at which beats the hammer of the collective conscience of humanity.[221]

*****

Almost five years after its creation, we still don't know who the secret big funders are who hide behind the public little ones, or where the money has really gone beyond the Wau Holland partial account. From insider accounts, we do know that the organization is in shambles:

> We stand by our assertions that Assange is responsible for gross financial mismanagement here at WIKILEAKS. Assange continues to enjoy a pretty good lifestyle, whilst claiming he receives no income from WIKILEAKS other than travelling expenses, and wait for it, air travel by coach class. Really Mr. Assange, enlighten us to just what other income streams you have, other than monies misappropriated from WIKILEAKS?
>
> Only a FULL AUDITED FINANCIAL DISCLOSURE of WIKILEAKS global donations and expenditures will finally reveal just how loose Assange has been with WIKILEAKS donor funding. As mentioned in our previous messages this need not compromise the safety of your sources or your staff. Contact GREENPEACE, they can provide you with some pointers in this regard.
>
> Illuminated by the spotlight of global publicity, Assange and Schmitt are trying to attempt to divert the WIKILEAKS donor base from the fact that there is no day to day accounting at WIKILEAKS. The LIMITED DISCLOSURE from the Wau Holland Foundation is no substitute for a fully audited disclosure of WIKILEAKS operating cash flows and current financial position.
>
> In our previous messages, we specifically stated that we were concerned about Assange's financial mismanagement of WIKILEAKS funds from April 2009 to April 2010; and year to date. None of these concerns has been addressed.
>
> The Wau Holland Foundation is in no position to provide a full accounting of WIKILEAKS current financial position for the simple reason it is not in full possession of the facts surrounding donations to WIKILEAKS namely:
>
> • The Wau Holland Foundation is totally unaware of monies received from WIKILEAKS non European con-

tributors. (source Wau Holland Foundation). This includes funding routed through Iceland.

• The Wau Holland Foundation is totally unaware of private or individual contributions to WIKILEAKS. (source Wau Holland Foundation)

• There is a very major disconnect concerning Assange's recent statements concerning donations (according to Assange, $1,000,000) and the Wau Holland Foundation limited financial disclosure.

We will have requested via Cryptome that they obtain such financial data from:

Wau Holland Stiftung
Postfach 640236
10048 Berlin
Tel: +49 40 401801 4665
vorstand[at]wau-holland-stiftung.de

a fully audited accounting for the periods detailed above. The Wau Holland Foundation has agreed to provide what data they have; subjected to request.

It is quite clear that WIKILEAKS finances are such that they can maintain their present WikiLeaks.org website in good condition, and be fit for purpose until the much promised upgrade; or movement to a new site. So why has it been abandoned Mr. Assange?

Finally, the Wau Foundations' limited financial release indicates that no money from European donors has been spent in the provision of a legal team for PFC Manning detained in Kuwait.

This completely supports our assertions concerning WIKILEAKS misrepresentation in recent emails that it required $50,000 in order to fly a legal team out to Kuwait. When in fact no one from WIKILEAKS has even met with Manning or anyone from the JAG office in KUWAIT.

WikiLeaks Insiders

AUTHENTICATION CODE

[Code omitted]

Julian Assange's very public fund raising campaign has effectively stalled with past and potential investors fading into the background. As previously indicated it is NOT the philosophy of WIKILEAKS that is in question, but Assange's credibility.[222]

The one individual who has stealthily appeared throughout the pages of this chapter, a word here, a mention there, a link to him through one of the characters on the Board of Directors, then he is gone ... only to reappear again a few lines later under a different guise is George Soros, who likes to sponsor ultra-left, subversive groups. In France, for example, the main left wing newspaper, *Liberación*, is owned by Baron Rothschild.

Soros' fingerprints are all over the WikiLeaks project. For example, not only has "Freedom House worked closely with Soros' Open Society Institutes ... in promoting such projects as the Washington-financed 2005 Tulip Revolution in Kyrgyzstan that brought the Washington-friendly dictator and drug boss, Kurmanbek Bakiyev to power,"[223] but WikiLeaks Board member, Ben Laurie, a former security boss of Google is a director of Open Rights Group, funded by Soros' front group, the Open Society Foundation. In a nutshell, WikiLeaks is packed with people who either work for Soros or are Soros' collaborators. We know that Open Society Foundation, was considered as one of the premier organizations to look to for funds.

> From:
> Sent: Thursday, December 28, 2006 2:58 PM
> To:
> Subject: Re: advisory board inquiry [Wikileaks]
>
> Hi xxxxxxxxxx. Thanks for your Soros suggestion. As you might know, one of the first things such organisatons look for is who is on your advisory board ;)
>

> So far, among the people who may be known to you, we have
xxxxxxxxxxxxxxxxxx, John Young, and xxxxxxxxxxxxxx and I
suspect Dan Ellsberg, but this has yet to be confirmed.
>
> On 12/29/06, xxxxxxxxxxxxxxxxxx wrote:
> > Thanks very much. I can see you have given this some seri-
ous thought, and I believe that I understand your argument.
I imagine that I am neither the first nor the last to raise questions.
> >
> > Anyway, I will continue to think about this, and let's see
how things unfold.
> >
> > One of your questions concerned possible funding sources.
One potential source might be the Soros Open Society Institute:
> >
> > http://www.soros.org/[224]

A word or two about Soros. To most people, George
Soros is a philanthropist, a man who donates hundreds of
millions of dollars to build a better world. A man of peace
and a man of freedom. A savvy investor and a businessman
with a Midas touch. However, a picture of the real Soros
is something quite different. He is, or rather his group of
foundations is, a front for the left-wing Anglo-American intelligence community on the one hand and the U.S. government's "Project Democracy" side on the other.

To understand how Soros is involved in WikiLeaks' disinformation campaign, it is imperative to know who George
Soros is and where he comes from. "Soros is no newcomer
to the world of criminal activity. He was handed his startup money by Baron Edmond de Rothschild's right-hand
man, George Karlweiss, who also launched the career of
fugitive narcotics trafficker, Robert Vesco. Since then, Soros has been involved in various vicious operations such as
financial speculative warfare to destroy national currencies,
pushing murderous 'useless eater' euthanasia polices, and
massively financing international campaigns for the legal-

ization of drugs." There is also a not so treasonous relationship of his with the Nazis during World War II.

Hector Rivas in his *Soros: Hit Man for the British Oligarchy* explains:

Soros began his genocidal legacy by working for the killing machine that slaughtered over 500,000 Hungarian Jews during the Holocaust. Young Soros was given the job of looting the properties of Jews under the regime of SS Lt. General Kurt Becher, head of the Waffen SS....

Prince Alexis Scherbatoff, former member of the U.S. Army Counterintelligence Corps before and after World War II, alleged that Soros obtained his first small fortune by selling his share of the loot seized by the Nazis....

On November 30, 1994, Soros spoke before an audience at the Columbia Presbyterian Medical Centre, and announced his new foundation, Project on Death in America, to shift the training of hospitals, nurses and doctors away from expensive life-saving treatment, to the proper care of the dying.... A Soros sponsored assisted suicide program to offer patients lethal prescriptions was the Oregon Death with Dignity Act.

Soros' promotion of narco-terrorism is the equivalent of the "gunboats" employed by the Empire in its launching of the 19th Century Opium Wars against China and India. One of the leading drug traffickers of the British Empire wrote that as long as drug use continues to dominate the country, "there is not the least reason to fear that she will become a military power of any importance, as the habit saps the energies and the vitality of the nation....

Soros ... is the front man for the Empire, covering up for the disgusting looting policy euphemistically known as globalization. Through organizations such as Human Rights Watch, the Soros Foundation and Open Society Institute, Soros pushes drugs and destroys nations.

Asserting that states have 'interests, but no principles,' Soros explains that the ideal open society would suppress particular national interests, while an international political and financial structure takes responsibility for the so-called common good.... Any nation that rejects glo-

95

balization, (i.e., British imperialism), is a closed society and subject to attacks from Soros and his shadow government of national agents.[225]

Again, the invisible hand of WikiLeaks is not too far away. What is needed to "open'" closed societies is an electronic trail of allegedly secret documents, whose secrets must be exposed for the good of "world peace," "democracy," and "Open Society."

THE SECRET OF QUANTUM FUND NV

"Soros is the visible side of a vast and nasty secret network of private financial interests, controlled by the leading aristocratic and royal families of Europe, centred in the British House of Windsor. This network, called by its members the Club of Isles, was built upon the wreckage of the British Empire after World War II...."[226]

According to the *American Almanac*, the bankers are part of a network called the "Club of the Isles" which is an informal association of European royalty including Queen Elizabeth. The Club of the Isles commands an estimated $10 trillion in assets. It lords over such corporate giants as Royal Dutch Shell, Imperial Chemical Industries, Lloyds of London, Unilever, Lonrho, Rio Tinto Zinc, and Anglo American DeBeers. It dominates the world supply of petroleum, gold, diamonds, and many other vital raw materials; and deploys these assets not merely in the pursuit of its geopolitical agenda.

> Rather than use the powers of the state to achieve their geopolitical goals, a secret cross-linked holding of private financial interests, tied to the old aristocratic oligarchy of Western Europe, was developed. It was in many ways modeled on the 17th-century British and Dutch East India Companies. The heart of this Club of the Isles is the financial center of the old British Empire, the City of London. Soros is one of what in medieval days were called

Hofjuden, the 'Court Jews,' who were deployed by the aristocratic families.

The most important of such 'Jews who are not Jews,' are the Rothschilds, who launched Soros' career. They are members of the Club of the Isles and retainers of the British royal family. This has been true since Amschel Rothschild sold the British Hessian troops to fight against George Washington during the American Revolution. "Soros is American only in his passport. He is a global financial operator, who happens to be in New York, simply because 'that's where the money is,' as the bank robber Willy Sutton once quipped, when asked why he always robbed banks. Soros speculates in world financial markets through his offshore company, Quantum Fund NV, a private investment fund, or "hedge fund." His hedge fund reportedly manages some $11-14 billion of funds on behalf of its clients, or investors---one of the most prominent of whom is, according to Soros, Britain's Queen Elizabeth, the wealthiest person in Europe....

Quantum Fund refers to the indeterminacy principle of Werner Heisenberg: the impossibility of simultaneously measuring the position and velocity of an atomic particle. Applied to the markets, the idea is that can not be reversed without affecting its prospects, for better or for worse. Soros option was both an ironic wink and a homage to the notions of fallibility, reflexivity and his own convention of incomplete determinism.

The Quantum Fund is registered in the tax haven of the Netherlands Antilles, in the Caribbean. This is to avoid paying taxes, as well as to hide the true nature of his investors and what he does with their money. In order to avoid U.S. government supervision of his financial activities, something normal U.S.-based investment funds must by law agree to in order to operate, Soros moved his legal headquarters to the Caribbean tax haven of Curacao. The Netherlands Antilles has repeatedly been cited by the Task Force on Money Laundering of the Organization for Economic Cooperation and Development (OECD) as one of the world's most important centers for laundering illegal proceeds of the Latin American cocaine and other drug traffic. It is a possession of the Netherlands....

George Soros is part of a tightly knit financial mafia---'mafia,' in the sense of a closed masonic-like fraternity of families pursuing common aims. Anyone who dares to criticize Soros or any of his associates, is immediately hit with the charge of being 'anti-Semitic'---- a criticism which often silences or intimidates genuine critics of Soros' unscrupulous operations. The Anti-Defamation League of B'nai B'rith considers it a top priority to "protect" Soros from the charges of 'anti-Semites' in Hungary and elsewhere in Central Europe, according to ADL National Director Abraham Foxman. The ADL's record of service to the British oligarchy has been amply documented by EIR.[227]

For a long time, the Anti-Defamation League was led by David Bialkin of the law firm Wilkie, Farr and Gallagher. "The ADL is a British intelligence operation founded in the United States by the British MI6 and controlled by Saul Steinberg and Eric Trist of Tavistock Institute. Saul Steinberg is the U.S. representative and partner to the Jacob de Rothschild family of London."[228]

"Soros' relation to the Rothschild finance circle represents no ordinary or casual banking connection. It goes a long way to explain the extraordinary success of a mere private speculator, and Soros' uncanny ability to 'gamble right' so many times in such high-risk markets. Soros has access to the 'insider track' in some of the most important government and private channels in the world...."[229]

Naturally, these links have been kept out of the public light in order to hide the true nature of Soros' relationship to the power circles in the City of London, Britain's Ministry of Foreign Affairs, Israel and U.S. financial circles.

(ENDNOTES)

1   *Brian Lehrer Live*, "WikiLeaks and Whistleblowers," CUNY-TV, March 31, 2010.

2   F. William Engdahl, "The Geopolitical Agenda behind the 2010 Nobel Peace Prize,"

oilgeopolitics.net, October 2010.

3   Michel Chossudovsky, "Who is behind WikiLeaks," globalresearch.ca, December, 13, 2001 http://www.globalresearch.ca/index.php?context=va&aid=22389.

4   Adam K. East, "The Anglo-American support apparatus behind the Afghani Mujahideen," *EIR*, October 13, 1995. http://www.larouchepub.com/other/1995/2241_mujahideen_control.html.

5   Ibid.

6   Michel Chossudovsky, "The Protest Movement in Egypt: 'Dictators' do not Dictate, They Obey Orders," globalresearch.ca, January 29,2011. http://www.globalresearch.ca/index.php?context=va&aid=22993.

7   F. William Engdahl, "The Geopolitical Agenda behind the 2010 Nobel Peace Prize," oilgeopolitics.net, October 2010. http://oilgeopolitics.net/Geopolitics___Eurasia/Nobel_Geopolitics/nobel_geopolitics.html.

8   Jeffrey Steinberg, "Neo-Cons Knee Deep inCaucasus Provocations," *EIR*, September 17, 2004.

9   F. William Engdahl, "The Geopolitical Agenda behind the 2010 Nobel Peace Prize," oilgeopolitics.net, October 2010.

10   Jeffrey Steinberg, "Neo-Cons Knee Deep in Caucasus Provocations," Sept 17, 2004, EIR. http://www.larouchepub.com/other/2004/3136neocons_caucasus.html.

11   Julie Lévesque, "Who's who at WikiLeaks," globalresearch.ca, December 20, 2010. http://www.globalresearch.ca/index.php?aid=22437&context=va.

12   http://cryptome.org/Wikileaks/wikileaks-leak.htm, email exchanges, January 2007.

13   Michel Chossudovsky, "The Protest Movement in Egypt: 'Dictators' do not Dictate, They Obey Orders," globalresearch.ca, January 29, 2011.

14   Adam K. East, "The Anglo-American support apparatus behind the Afghani mujahideen," *EIR*, October 13, 1995.

15   Michel Chossudovsky, "The Protest Movement in Egypt: 'Dictators' do not Dictate, They Obey Orders," globalresearch.ca, January 29, 2011.

16   Stephen Gowans, "The NED, Tibet, North Korea and Zimbabwe," What's left, March 22, 2010, http://gowans.wordpress.com/2010/03/22/the-ned-tibet-north-korea-and-zimbabwe/.

17   Adam K. East, "The Anglo-American support apparatus behind the Afghani mujahideen," *EIR*, October 13, 1995.

18   Ibid.

19   Ibid.

20   Ibid.

21   Ibid.

22   Ibid.

23   Ibid.

24   Jeanne Whalen, David Crawford, "How WikiLeaks keeps its funding secret," WSJ.com, August 23, 2010. http://online.wsj.com/article/SB10001424052748704554104575436231926853198.html.

25   Michel Chossudovsky, "Who is behind WikiLeaks," globalresearch.ca, December, 13, 2001.

26   Ibid.

27   "WikiLeaks' Avisory Board." http://web.archive.org/web/20080327225000/www.Wikileaks.org/wiki/Advisory_Board, WikiLeaks.org, 27 March 2008.

28   http://www.entertainoz.com.au/Speakers-Bureau/Speakers/Phillip-Adams.

29   Julie Lévesque, "Who is who at WikiLeaks," globalresearch.ca, December 20, 2010.

30   David Kushner, "Inside WikiLeaks' Leak Factory," *Mother Jones*, 6 April, 2010. http://motherjones.com/politics/2010/04/wikileaks-julian-assange-iraq-video?page=2

31   Ellen Nakashima, Google to enlist NSA to help it ward off cyberattacks, *Washington Post*, February 4, 2010. http://www.commondreams.org/headline/2010/02/04-6.

32   http://www.openrightsgroup.org/people/board

33   http://www.openrightsgroup.org/ourwork/annual-reports/annual-report-2010/finances-and-governance.

34   F. William Engdahl, "The Secret Financial Network Behind 'Wizard' George Soros," EIR, Nov 1, 1996. http://www.questionsquestions.net/docs04/engdahl-soros.html.

35   http://web.archive.org/web/20080327225000/www.Wikileaks.org/wiki/Advisory_Board.

36   Julie Lévesque, Who is who at WikiLeaks, globalresearch.ca, December 20, 2010.

37   F. William Engdahl, "The Geopolitical Agenda behind the 2010 Nobel Peace Prize," October 2010.

38   Julie Lévesque, "Who is who at WikiLeaks," globalresearch.ca, December 20, 2010

39   Scott Creighton, "If We Lose our Internet Freedoms Because of WikiLeaks, You Should At Least Know Why," globalresearch.ca, December 11, 2010.

40   Jonathan Mirsky, "Directives from China's Ministry of Truth on Liu Xiaobo winning Nobel, Democracy Digest, words can be fatal in China," October 8, 2010.

41   Julie Lévesque, "Who is who at WikiLeaks," globalresearch.ca, December 20, 2010

42   http://www.rferl.org/section/history/133.html.

43   WikiLeaks' Avisory Board, http://web.archive.org/web/20080327225000/www.Wikileaks.org/wiki/Advisory_Board WikiLeaks.org, 27 March 2008.

44   Charles Tuttle and Marcia Merry Baker, "The Cartel 'Experts' Decide Who Eats," *EIR*, December 8, 1995.

45   EIR Investigative Team, The Genocidal Lombard League of Cities Apparatus, June 6, 2008, p. 61.

46   Daniel Estulin, *Shadow Masters*, TrineDay, 2010, p. 51.

47   EIR Investigative Team, "The Genocidal Lombard League of Cities Apparatus," June 6, 2008, p. 61. http://www.larouchepub.com/eiw/public/2008/2008_20-29/2008_20-29/2008-21/pdf/50-51_3521.pdf.

48   Ibid. pp. 50-55.

49   Charles Tuttle and Marcia Merry Baker, "The Cartel 'Experts' Decide Who Eats," *EIR*, December 8, 1995.

50   Julie Lévesque, "Who is who at WikiLeaks," globalresearch.ca, December 20, 2010.

51   Ibid.

52   F. William Engdahl, "The Geopolitical Agenda behind the 2010 Nobel Peace Prize," oilgeopolitics.net, October 2010.

53   Ibid.

54   CBC News – Website wants to take whistleblowing online, January 11, 2007. http://www.cbc.ca/news/story/2007/01/11/wikileaks-whistle.html.

55   Ibid.

56   Michio Kaku and Daniel Axelrod, *To Win a Nuclear War: The Pentagon's Secret War Plans*, South End Press, 1999, p. 30.

57   F. William Engdahl, *Full Spectrum Dominance*, Third Millennium Press May, 2009.

58   Ibid.

59   Michel Chossudovsky, Who is behind WikiLeaks, www.globalresearch.ca, December 13, 2010.

60   "Russia and Iran to Enhance Ties," *Global Ties*, January 19, 2011 http://world.glo-

baltimes.cn/europe/2011-01/614053.html.

61   Stephen C. Webster, "Russian WikiLeaks comes under attack over photos alleg-
      edly showing Putin's 'palace,'" *Raw Story*, January 19, 2011. http://www.rawstory.
      com/rs/2011/01/19/russian-official-praised-assange-russia-blocks-wikileaks-
      photos-putins-mansion/.

62   Stephen C. Webster, "Russian WikiLeaks comes under attack over photos alleg-
      edly showing Putin's 'palace,'" *Raw Story*, January 19, 2011.

63   William Norman Grigg, "Behind the bias: instead of investigating and exposing
      the actions of the power elite, the major media are complicit in that elite's drive for
      total control," *The New American*, February 10, 2003.

64   Ibid.

65   Matthew d'Ancona, "After this, we can't believe a word you say, Gordon Brown,"
      The Telegraph, March 9, 2008.

66   William Norman Grigg, "Behind the bias: instead of investigating and exposing
      the actions of the power elite, the major media are complicit in that elite's drive for
      total control," *The New American*, February 10, 2003.

67   Mary Louise, "Operation Mockingbird: CIA Media Manipulation," http://www.
      prisonplanet.com/analysis_louise_01_03_03_mockingbird.html,   prisonplanet.
      com.

68   William Norman Grigg, "Behind the bias: instead of investigating and exposing
      the actions of the power elite, the major media are complicit in that elite's drive for
      total control," *The New American*, February 10, 2003.

69   Ibid.

70   John Galt, "Beating the New World Order," http://www.knowfree.com/beating.
      htm.

71   Servando Gonzalez, "A Chronology of Treason," http://www.intelinet.org/sg_site/
      articles/sg_chronology_of_treason.html, May 20, 2008.

72   William Norman Grigg, "Behind the bias: instead of investigating and exposing
      the actions of the power elite, the major media are complicit in that elite's drive for
      total control," *The New American*, February 10, 2003.

73   Ibid.

74   http://www.cfr.org/about/membership/roster.html?letter=S.

75   Michel Chossudovsky, "Who is behind WikiLeaks?" Globalresearch.ca, Decem-
      ber13, 2010.

76   Andrew Gavin Marshall, "America's Strategic Repression of the 'Arab Awakening'
      Part 2," globalresearch.ca, February 9, 2011.

77   *Aid & Abet*, Vol. 2, No.2, pg. 7.

78   William Norman Grigg, "Behind the bias: instead of investigating and exposing
      the actions of the power elite, the major media are complicit in that elite's drive for
      total control," *The New American*, February 10, 2003.

79   Ibid.

80   Ibid.

81   Laughland, John, "Fill Full the Mouth of Famine," *Scoop Independent News*, July 29,
      2004.

82   Keith Harmon Snow, "Oil in Darfur? Special Ops in Somalia?" Global Research,
      February 7, 2007. http://www.globalresearch.ca/index.php?context=va&aid=4717.

83   William Norman Grigg, "Behind the bias: instead of investigating and exposing
      the actions of the power elite, the major media are complicit in that elite's drive for
      total control," *The New American*, February 10, 2003.

84   Ibid.

85   Ibid.

86   Mary Louise, "Operation Mockingbird: CIA Media Manipulation," http://www.
      prisonplanet.com/analysis_louise_01_03_03_mockingbird.html.

87   William Norman Grigg, "Behind the bias: instead of investigating and exposing
      the actions of the power elite, the major media are complicit in that elite's drive for
      total control," *The New American*, February 10, 2003.

88   Michel Chossudovsky, "Who is behind WikiLeaks," globalresearch.ca, December
      13, 2010.

89   Scott Creighton, "If We Lose our Internet Freedoms Because of WikiLeaks, You
      Should At Least Know Why," globalresearch.ca, December 11, 2010.

90   Ibid.

91   Tracy Samantha Schmidt, "A Wiki for Whistle-Blowers, *Time* magazine,
      Jan.   22,   2007.   http://www.time.com/time/nation/article/0,8599,1581189,00.
      html#ixzz1ExtfiKg4.

92   Scott Creighton, "If We Lose our Internet Freedoms Because of WikiLeaks, You
      Should At Least Know Why," globalresearch.ca, December 11, 2010.

93   Tracy Samantha Schmidt, "A Wiki for Whistle-Blowers," *Time* magazine,
      Jan.   22,   2007.   http://www.time.com/time/nation/article/0,8599,1581189,00.
      html#ixzz1ExtfiKg4

94   Ibid, quoting http://mirror.Wikileaks.info/.

95   Michel Chossudovsky, "Who is Behind WikiLeaks?," www.globaresearch.ca, De-
      cember 10, 2010.

96   Ibid.

97   Ibid.

98   Ibid.

99   "'The *Economist*' Spills the beans," *EIR* editorial, p.65, February 16, 2007.

100   Michel Chossudovsky, "Who is Behind WikiLeaks?" www.globaresearch.ca, De-
      cember 10, 2010.

101   Jeffrey Steinberg and Pierre Beaudry, "Rohatyn's Fascist Roots Are
      Showing," *EIR*, June 30, 2006 http://www.larouchepub.com/eiw/pub-
      lic/2006/2006_20-29/2006_20-29/2006-26/pdf/17-18_626_feathist.pdf.

102   Ibid.

103   Michel Chossudovsky, "Who is Behind WikiLeaks?" www.globaresearch.ca, De-
      cember 10, 2010.

104   Ibid.

105   Ibid.

106   Ibid.

107   David Guyatt, "Subverting the Media," deepblacklies.co.uk, undated.

108   Mary Louise, "Operation Mockingbird: CIA Media Manipulation," http://www.
      prisonplanet.com/analysis_louise_01_03_03_mockingbird.html.

109   David Guyatt, "Subverting the Media," deepblacklies.co.uk, undated.

110   Alex Constantine, "The Depraved Spies and Moguls of the CIA's Operation
      MOCKINGBIRD," Tales from the Crypt. http://whatreallyhappened.com/RAN-
      CHO/POLITICS/MOCK/mockingbird.php.

111   David Guyatt, "Subverting the Media," www.deepblacklies.co.uk.

112   Ibid.

113   Ibid.

114   Michel Chossudovsky, "Who is Behind WikiLeaks?" www.globaresearch.ca, De-
      cember 10, 2010.

115   Chaim Kupferberg, "The Propaganda Preparation of 9/11," Global Research, Sep-
      tember 19, 2002.

116   Michel Chossudovsky, Who is Behind WikiLeaks? globalresearch.ca, December

10, 2010.

117 Ibid.

118 F. William Engdahl, "Something stinks about WikiLeaks," oilgeopolitics.net, November 8, 2010.

119 Scott Creighton, "If We Lose our Internet Freedoms Because of WikiLeaks, You Should At Least Know Why," globalresearch.ca, December 10, 2010.124; Julie Lévesque, "Who is who at WikiLeaks," globalresearch.ca, December 20, 2010.

120 Ibid.

121 Julie Lévesque, "Who is who at WikiLeaks," globalresearch.ca, December 20, 2010.

122 Peiter "Mudge" Zatko, "Information Security Expert Who Warned that Hackers 'Could Take Down the Internet in 30 Minutes' Returns to BBN Technologies," *Business Wire*, 1 February 2005.

123 Julie Lévesque, "Who is who at WikiLeaks," globalresearch.ca, December 20, 2010.

124 Ibid.

125 http://www.darpa.mil/mission.html.

126 Gareth Cook, "Defending Darpa The Government's Strangest Research Might Be Its Best," *Boston Globe*, August 3, 2003, p. E1.

127 Oyang Teng, "Video Games and the Wars of the Future," *EIR*, August 10 2007.

128 Ibid.

129 Ibid.

130 Julie Lévesque, "Who is who at WikiLeaks," December 20, 2010, globalresearch.ca.

131 Wayne Madsen, Arthur Zbygniew, "Is WikiLeaks Part of U.S. Cyber-Warfare Operations?" http://arthurzbygniew.blogspot.com/2010/03/soros-co-back-wikileaks-kosher-mob-oval.html.

132 "WikiLeaks crippled, can't protect leakers anonymity," Reuters, February 13, 2011.

133 Interview with *Russia Today*, John Young, January 2, 2011.

134 John Young, interviewed on *Brian Lehrer TV Show*, CUNY TV. April 2010 http://vimeo.com/10615688.

135 Interview with *Russia Today*, John Young, January 2, 2011.

136 Ibid.

137 Julie Lévesque, "Who is who at WikiLeaks," globalresearch.ca. December 20, 2010.

138 Scott Creighton, "An Open Letter to Glenn Greenwald on the Subject of WikiLeaks: Just... Stop," www.willyloman.wordpress.com, January 1, 2011.

139 Andrew Orlowski, "WikiLeaks are for-hire mercenaries – Cryptome," *The Register*, December 7, 2010.

140 http://cryptome.org/0001/wikileaks-funds.htm.

141 http://www.mediagiraffe.org/mgprofiles/index.php?action=profile&id=458.

142 http://diswww.mit.edu/menelaus/bt/204.

143 http://nssdc.gsfc.nasa.gov/nssdc_news/june95/09_v_thomas_0695.html.

144 Julie Lévesque, "Who is who at WikiLeaks," globalresearch.ca, December 20, 2010.

145 Ibid.

146 Raffi Khatchadourian, "No Secrets," *The New Yorker*, June 7, 2010.

147 Webster Tarpley, interview with Alex Jones, prisonplanet.com, December 5, 2010.

148 Mark Phillips, "Operation Monarch," *Outpost of Freedom*, February 3, 1993.

149 "The Phoenix Project, Use Of Monarch Mind Control Methodology For Programming Manchurian Candidates For Social Violence In U.S. Society," A Newsletter From A Christian Ministry, December 1993.

150 Michael A. Hoffman II, *Secret Societies and Psychological Warfare*, Independent History and Research, pp. 91-95.

151 Peter Levenda, *Sinister Forces, Book I: The Nine*, TrineDay, 2005, p .xx.

152   Ibid, p. 217, 2005.

153   Ibid, p. 218.

154   Ibid, p. 229.

155   Ibid, p. 227-229.

156   http://cryptome.org/Wikileaks/wikileaks-leak2.htm.

157   Peter Levenda, *Sinister Forces, Book I: The Nine*, Trineday-2005, p.229 & 230.

158   Ibid, p.227 & 229.

159   Heather Marsh, "Who Were WikiLeaks?" GeorgiesBC's Blog, December 2, 2010. Quoting Assange. http://georgiebc.wordpress.com/2010/12/02/who-were-wikileaks/.

160   http://cryptome.org/Wikileaks/wikileaks-leak2.htm.

161   http://cryptome.org/Wikileaks/wikileaks-leak.htm.

162   "Wanted by the CIA: The man who keeps no secrets," *The Independent* July 18, 2010.

163   Ibid.

164   Ronald West, "Julian Assange, Agent Provocateur," alternet.org, October 11, 2010.

165   Daniel Estulin, "Bilderberg report 2005, Rottach-Egern," *Nexus Magazine*, Sept 2005.

166   Julie Lévesque, "Who is Who at WikiLeaks," globalresearch.ca, December 20, 2010.

167   WikiLeaks.org.

168   "Orcinus," "Those awful, mean 'Bush haters," http://dneiwert.blogspot.com/2003/08/those-awful-mean-bush-haters.html, August 23, 2003.

169   Ibid.

170   WikiLeaks.org, 17, December 2007.

171   Julie Lévesque, "Who is who at WikiLeaks," December 20, 2010, globalresearch.ca.

172   Daniel Tenser, "Obama Staffer Calls for 'Cognitive Infiltration' of '9/11 Conspiracy Groups', *RawStory*, January 15, 2010.

173   Michel Chossudovsky, "Manufacturing dissent: the anti-globalization movement is funded by the corporate elite," globalresearch.ca, September 21, 2010.

174   Michel Chossudovsky, "Who is behind WikiLeaks?" globalresearch.ca, december 13, 2010.

175   Dr. Mohammad Omar Farooq, "Tyranny and the Tyrants – The unlearned lessons of history," iviews.com, September 11, 2005.

176   Brian Boyd, "Vladimir Nabokov – The American Years," Princeton University Press, 1991, p. 97.

177   William Engdahl, "Hidden Intelligence Operation Behind the WikiLeaks Release of 'Secret' Documents?," globalresearch.ca, August 12, 2010.

178   Ibid.

179   Ibid.

180   Tony Papert, "Degenerates surround a Nero-like President," *EIR*, April 24, 2009, p. 65.

181   Ibid.

182   John Hoefle, "Clean out the nest of psywar vipers around Nero Obama," *EIR*, October 19, 2009.

183   Ibid.

184   Ibid.

185   Ibid.

186   "The Coming Fall of the House of Windsor," Slide Show, *The New Federalist*, 1994.

187   Helga Zepp-LaRouche, "The Historical Roots of Green Fascism," The Schiller In-

stitute, April 13, 2007.

188   Friedrich Georg Jünger, *The Perfection of Technology*, Regnery Pub 1982.

189   Daniel Estulin, "Towards One world Company Ltd, Press Conference," European Parliament, June 1, 2010.

190   Helga Zepp-Larouche, "The Historic Roots of Green Fascism," The Schiller Institute, April 13, 1982.

191   Ibid.

192   Bertrand Russell, *The Impact of Science on Society*, Allen & Unwin 1952.

193   Helga Zepp-Larouche, "The Historic Roots of Green Fascism," The Schiller Institute, April 13, 1982.

194   John Hoefle, "Clean out the nest of psywar vipers around Nero Obama," *EIR*, October 19, 2009.

195   Ibid.

196   Ibid.

197   Richard Stengel, Transcript: *Time* interview with WikiLeaks' Julian Assange, *Time* magazine, 30 November 2010: http://news.yahoo.com/s/time/20101201/wl_time/08599203404000.

198   Ibid.

199   John Hoefle, "Clean out the nest of psywar vipers around Nero Obama," *EIR*, October 19, 2009.

200   Tony Papert, "Degenerates surround a Nero-like President," April 24, 2009, p.65.

201   John Hoefle, "Clean out the nest of psywar vipers around Nero Obama," *EIR*, October 19, 2009.

202   New 'Pecora Hearings' Target:The Slush Fund of the Summers Gang, EIRNS, April 17, 2009.

203   Julie Lévesque, "Who is who at WikiLeaks," globalresearch.ca, December 20, 2010.

204   Andy Greenberg, "An Interview with WikiLeaks' Julian Assange," *Forbes*, 29 October, 2010.

205   "The secret life of Julian Assange," CNN, 2 December 2010.

206   Julie Lévesque, "Who is who at WikiLeaks," globalresearch.ca, December 20, 2010.

207   Ibid.

208   http://cryptome.org/0001/mj-wl-show.htm.

209   Andrew Orlowski, "WikiLeaks are for-hire mercenaries – Cryptome," *The Register*, December 7, 2010.

210   http://cryptome.org/0001/wikileaks-funds.htm, May 16, 2010.

211   Ibid.

212   Andrew Orlowski, "WikiLeaks are for-hire mercenaries – Cryptome," *The Register*, December 7, 2010.

213   John Young, interview with Alex Jones, prisonplanet.com, February 26, 2010.

214   Stephanie Strom, "Pentagon Sees a Threat From Online Muckrackers," *New York Times*, March 17, 2010.

215   http://www.reddit.com/r/politics/comments/bmx4g/cryptome_on_wikileaks/.

216   http://rt.com/usa/news/bradley-manning-wikileaks-protest/print/.

217   "A WikiLeaks Insider," http://cryptome.org/0001/wikileaks-funds.htm.

218   http://cryptome.org/0003/wikileaks-lash.htm.

219   Andrew Orlowski, "WikiLeaks are for-hire mercenaries – Cryptome," *The Register*, December 7, 2010.

220   Cryptome.org, http://cryptome.org/Wikileaks/wikileaks-leak.htm.

221   http://www.cryptome.org/0001/wikileaks-costs.htm.

222   http://www.cryptome.org/0001/wikileaks-funds.htm.

223   F. William Engdahl, "The Geopolitical Agenda behind the 2010 Nobel Peace Prize," Oilgeopolitics.net, October 2010.

224   http://www.openrightsgroup.org/ourwork/annual-reports/annual-report-2010/finances-and-governance.

225   Hector A. Rivas Jr., "George Soros: Hit-man for the British Oligarchy," July 4, 2008, *EIR*, p.65.

226   F. William Engdahl, "The Secret Financial Network Behind 'Wizard' George Soros," *EIR*, November 1, 1996.

227   Ibid.

228   John Coleman, *The Conspirators' Hierarchy: The Committee of 300*, 4th edition, p.184.

229   William F. Engdahl, "The Secret Financial Network Behind "Wizard" George Soros," *EIR*, November 1, 1996.

Chapter 2

Afghanistan –
Disinformation Made to Order

"WikiLeaks is upheld as a breakthrough in the battle against media disinformation and the lies of the US government; an immeasurable victory against corporate media censorship."[1] According to the *Guardian*, "US authorities have known for weeks that they have suffered a hemorrhage of secret information on a scale which makes even the leaking of the Pentagon Papers during the Vietnam war look limited by comparison."[2]

In July 2010, WikiLeaks released between 75,000 and 90,000 pages of documents that "exhaustively chronicle the twists, turns and horror of the 9-year-old war in Afghanistan."[3] Unquestionably, the released documents have provoked unparalleled global interest as well as an important and valuable data bank. The documents provide "a useful window into the manner in which the ... international financial oligarchy operates. The oligarchy [in question], is essentially a private criminal enterprise, which stretches across the globe, operating through a network of government agencies, private institutions, and both publicly owned and private corporations. Some of these relationships are out in the open, while others are hidden.... The ... historic role in the Asian opium trade is a good example of how the oligarchy functions."[4] We will be examining it in this chapter.

The WikiLeak documents date from between 2004 and January 2010, are divided into more than 100 categories and cover much of what the public already knows about the troubled nine-year conflict. "Tens of thousands of pages of reports document attacks on U.S. troops and their responses, relations between Americans in the field and their Afghan allies, intramural squabbles among Afghan civilians and security forces, and concerns about neighboring Pakistan's ties to the Taliban."[5]

However, there are several things that need to be kept in mind. Because these are not paper documents but digital files, we can't know for sure if they are authentic. There are three versions in major newspapers, all digital, which are notoriously easy to doctor. And apparently, according to insiders, the files are made in the field on computers and sent in to headquarters. So, when we are told, "this the biggest dump of military documents," that is not totally honest because these are not actual paper documents. Plus many intelligence agencies are also dumping huge amounts of files onto the Internet.

Cryptome is a "repository for information about freedom of speech, cryptography, spying, and surveillance."[6] Cryptome's founder is an independent scholar and architect John Young. According to Young, "when studying the WikiLeaks War Logs, bear in mind that intelligence streams – hardcopy, digital, electromagnetic – are salted with spurious entries as markers to authenticate the stream, identify disruptions and unauthorised plants, direct the product to various collectors with varying levels of classification, and more. The spurious entries will not be distinguishable from the other material, it is their positions in the stream, or omissions from the stream, which will be part of authentication. None of this requires or is protected by encryption, indeed, encryption is customarily used to mislead about other means and methods – which is why it is so loudly touted.

> Some streams are entirely spurious but composed of authentic material, to cloud the process, to entrap, to delude, to fake a vulnerability. These methods are well known to the 'techheads' of WikiLeaks although they

may lack required programs and equipment to analyze streams in all their guises. WikiLeaks claims to cloud its transmissions for protection, a perfect marker for others. Three versions of the Afghan War logs were given to the dupes, another to the public. Another for WikiLeaks alone, more or less.[7]

Before the Afghanistan data dump, WikiLeaks had used digital signature on documents to prove authentication. But not this time. Also, for the first time, WikiLeaks released these documents to major media before the general public.

Let's move to the documents themselves. The 90,000 low-level intelligence interoffice, routine documents, obtained by WikiLeaks and made available to a number of mainstream news organizations, focus their coverage on two things: Pakistan is treacherous and Pakistan betrayed the United States. "Reports of this nature serve to provide legitimacy to US drone attacks against alleged terrorist targets inside Pakistan,"[8] and the demonization of Pakistani intelligence service, ISI.

Furthermore, "the corporate media's use and interpretation of the WikiLeaks cables serves to uphold two related myths: 1) Iran has nuclear weapons program and constitutes a threat to global security. 2) Saudi Arabia and Pakistan are state sponsors of several Islamic terrorist organizations, a fact that is known to all informed observers and amply documented. They are financing Islamic terrorist organizations, which are intent upon attacking the US and its NATO allies."[9]

What the WikiLeaks reports fail to mention, however, is that historically US intelligence has used Pakistan and Saudi Arabia intelligence to hide its support for terrorist organizations. These may well be US sponsored intelligence operations using Saudi and Pakistani intelligence as intermediaries.

And as Arundhati Roy, winner of the Booker Prize for her novel, *The God of Small Things* writes in "War is Peace": "Setting aside the rhetoric for a moment, consider the fact that the world has not yet found an acceptable definition of 'terrorism.' One country's terrorist is too often another's freedom fighter. At the heart of the matter lies the world's deep-seated ambivalence towards violence. Once violence is accepted as a legitimate political instrument, then the morality and political acceptability of terrorists (insurgents or freedom fighters) becomes contentious, bumpy terrain. The U.S. government itself has funded, armed, and sheltered plenty of rebels and insurgents around the world. The CIA and Pakistan's Inter-Services Intelligence agency trained and armed the mujahideen who, in the 1980s, were seen as terrorists by the government in Soviet-occupied Afghanistan.

"While President Reagan posed with them for a group portrait and called them the moral equivalents of America's founding fathers. Today, Pakistan – America's ally in this new war – sponsors insurgents who cross the border into Kashmir in India. Pakistan lauds them as 'freedom fighters,' India calls them 'terrorists.' India, for its part, denounces countries who sponsor and abet terrorism, but the Indian army has, in the past, trained separatist Tamil rebels (LTTE) asking for a homeland in Sri Lanka, who are responsible for countless acts of bloody terrorism. (Just as the CIA abandoned the mujahideen after they had served its purpose, India abruptly turned its back on the Tamil rebels for a host of political reasons. It was an enraged LTTE suicide-bomber who assassinated former Indian prime minister Rajiv Gandhi in 1991.)"[10]

Economist Michel Chossudovsky raises some interesting issues when he writes that the use of the WikiLeaks documents by the media "sustains the illusion that the CIA has nothing to do with the terror network and that Saudi Arabia and the Gulf states are 'providing the lion's share of funding' to al Qaeda, the Taliban, Lashkar-e-Taiba, among others, when in fact this financing is undertaken in liaison and consultation with their US intelligence counterparts."[11] This, it should be understood, is "war on terror" propaganda.

The real story is quite different. "Largely as a result of the Bush administration's 'war on terror,'" write Elizabeth Gould & Paul Fitzgerald, "the traditional framework of the East-West political dialogue has broken and fallen entirely under the spell of the extremists on both sides. Since much of the West's relationship was based on Cold War and Neo-colonial relationships to begin with it shouldn't come as a surprise that it finally broke. Yet nothing new and as powerful has come along to replace it. Now what we see is confusion in the West as declining powers like the U.S. attempt to rig the international system to ensure some role in a future where they cannot control events as they had. The U.S. failure in Afghanistan is largely due to an inability to switch its thinking from the Cold War to a multi-polar world while it had the authority and power to do so. Instead, as the result of manipulation by right wing and neo-conservative intellectuals, the U.S. simply substituted Islam for communism and went on with an aggressive strategy as before."[12]

> In regards to Pakistan, while it is important to be highly critical of the validity of the 'perspectives' within the cables in regards to Pakistan and the Taliban, since Pakistan is a current and escalating target in the 'War [of] Terror,' there are things to keep in mind: historically, the Pakistani ISI has funded, armed and trained the Taliban, but always with U.S. assistance and support. Thus, we must examine the situation presently and so historically. WikiLeaks revealed, that Arab Gulf states help fund the Taliban in Afghanistan, so the common claim that it is Pakistan 'alone' is immediately made to be erroneous. Is it possible that Pakistan is still working with the Taliban? Of course. They have historically through their intelligence services, the ISI, and while they have never done it without U.S. support (mostly through the CIA), the ISI still receives most of its outside funding from the CIA. The CIA funding of the ISI, a reality since the late 70s, picked up dramatically following 9/11, the operations of which the ISI has been itself complicit in financing. Thus,

the CIA rewarded the financiers of 9/11 by increasing their funds.

The trouble with discounting information that does not fit in with your previously conceived ideas is that it does not allow for evolution or progress in thinking. This should never be done in regards to any subject, yet it is commonly done for all subjects, by official and critical voices alike. With Pakistan, we must understand that while historically it has been a staunch U.S. ally in the region, propping up every government, supporting every coup, American geopolitical ambitions have changed as a result of the changing geopolitical reality of the world. Pakistan has drawn increasingly close to China, which built a major seaport on Pakistan's coast, giving China access to the Indian Ocean. This is a strategic threat to India and the United States more broadly, which seeks to subdue and control China's growing influence (while simultaneously attempting to engage in efforts of international integration with China, specifically economically). India and Pakistan are historical enemies, and wars have been fought between them before. India and America are in a strategic alliance, and America helped India with its nuclear program, much to the distaste of the Pakistanis, who drew closer to China. Pakistan occupies an area of the utmost strategic importance: with its neighbors being Afghanistan, China, India and Iran.[13]

In her *Outlook* article, "War is Peace," Arundhati Roy follows up: "It is important for governments and politicians to understand that manipulating these huge, raging human feelings for their own narrow purposes may yield instant results, but eventually and inexorably, they have disastrous consequences. Igniting and exploiting religious sentiments for reasons of political expediency is the most dangerous legacy that governments or politicians can bequeath to any people – including their own. People who live in societies ravaged by religious or communal bigotry know that every religious text – from the Bible to the Bhagwad Gita – can be mined and misinterpreted to justify anything, from nuclear war to genocide to corporate globalization."[14] But this is just the tip of the iceberg. There also seems to be a great deal of whitewashing of valuable information that doesn't fit into a pre-determined mold, set up by the mainstream press. As Andrew Gavin Marshall writes at globalresearch.ca: "The 'revelations' however, are not simply challenging American perceptions of America, but of all nations and their populations."[15] And to the would-be-Masters of the Universe, this lack of control is unnerving. "This is likely why the corporate media is so heavily involved in the dissemination of this information."[16] In other words, they are heavily involved in the interpretation of the message. For example, historical and cultural differences between ethnic groups are simply chalked up to local al-Qaeda cells, if we are to believe WikiLeaks.

A key area that offers misleading interpretation in the mainstream press is the Balochistan street violence supposedly orchestrated by local terrorist elements with close links to al-Qaeda. However, to understand the massacres of Shiites in Karbala, Baghdad and in Pakistan's Balochistan province of Quetta during the procession of Muhurrum on March 2, 2004 and its implications in the War on Terror today, we must go back to the creation of Pakistan in 1947. B. Raman, writing for *Kashmir Telegraph*, explains that when Pakistan was founded that year:

> ... the Shia [Shiites] were amongst the major land-owners of Pakistan's Punjab, its granary, and many of the Sunnis, who migrated to Pakistan from India's Punjab, were largely poor landless farm workers, who had to earn their livelihood in their country of adoption by working in the farms of the Shias....
>
> Clearly the exploitation of Sunnis by Shiite landowners triggered the polarization between the two Islamic sects in Pakistan. The race to sectarian rivalry began when Shiite elements founded Tehrik Nifaz-i-Fiqah-i-Jafri (TNFJ, meaning the Movement for the Implementation of Fiqah-i-Jafri, Shia school of Islamic jurisprudence,

which later became known as the Tehrik-e-Jaffri Pakistan). In response to this attempt of a minority to impose their ideas on the majority, Maulana Haq Nawaz Jhangvi, a Deobandi cleric (a sub-sect within Sunni) founded in Jhang, a Punjab district of Pakistan, a Sunni extremist organization called Anjuman Sipah-i-Sahaba Pakistan (ASSP), which later was renamed Sipah-e-Sahaba Pakistan (SSP). This organization became a political organization that apparently also has a terrorist wing, while its offshoot, the Lashkar-e-Jhangvi (LEJ), is a hardened terrorist group.

With the blessing of Zia-ul-Haq, Pakistan's military dictator in the 1980s, the SSP questioned women's right to lead the country and spread the message that the Shiites and Nusrat Bhutto, Benazir's mother, were Iran's subordinates. Furthermore, the SSP demanded that the Shiites be denied Muslim identity while politically pushing the agenda of turning Pakistan into a Sunni state. SSP's virulently anti-Shiite ideology was also exploited by Iraq and U.S. intelligence agencies in their attempts to destabilize Iran and create the conditions to overthrow Shiite clerics in power in Tehran. As a result of support from Saddam Hussein in the 90s, SSP, a Pakistani anti-Shia movement and not anti-Iranian, began to harass Iranians who lived and visited Pakistan.

Many known Pakistani and Arab terrorists began their careers as members of the SSP network and took part in the massacres of Shiites in Pakistan, Iran and Afghanistan. One of them for example, is Ramzi Yousef, the mastermind of the attack on the Twin Towers in 1993. Another was Maulana Masood Azhar of Jaish-e-Mohammad (JEM), a religious leader who supports Muslim separatists fighting in the conflict zone of Kashmir, or Abu Musab al-Zarqawi, a Jordanian accused of being the mastermind behind a string of spectacular suicide bombings in Iraq. Along with other Jordanians, most of Chechen blood, Al-Zarqawi came to Pakistan in the 1980s to join the Arab mercenary force trained and supplied by the CIA and Pakistani intelligence service (ISI) to be used against Soviet troops in Afghanistan.[17]

Consequently, during the 1980s, a sophisticated network between Afghan mujahideen, and religious groups from Pakistan was launched. This network was equipped with a generous supply of arms from the US, the UK, Israel and South Africa. The mix of easy access to weapons with an increasingly motivated group of terrorists meant a rapid spread of violence from Afghanistan to Pakistan itself. The growing extremism among rival militant groups increased tensions due to the widespread western support of Afghan groups fighting the Soviets and then to the support of specific groups of hard-line Islamists, after the Soviet withdrawal turned into full-blown carnage. First a "civil war" between the mujahideen fighters themselves, then later war against the CIA and the United States government.

Raman continues, "Zarqawi, along with the late Riaz Basra, the leader of the Lashkar-e-Jhangvi (LEJ), the militant wing of the SSP, helped the Taliban in the capture of Kabul in September, 1996.... Osama bin Laden never liked Saddam, whom he looked upon as an apostate because of his secular and socialist policies, and the proximity of the LEJ and al-Zarqawi to Saddam's intelligence agency created differences between them and bin Laden."[18]

Up until 2002, LEJ's activities against Shiites focused only in the Punjab and Sindh. The province of Balochistan, which covers a huge area in southwestern Pakistan, bordering Afghanistan and Iran remained fairly free of anti-Shia sentiment. That changed with the arrest by Pakistani authorities in March 2003 of Khalid Sheikh Mohammad (KSM), allegedly one of the 9/11 conspirators and his subsequent hand-over to the FBI. It was rumored that KSM had fled to Quetta from Karachi in September 2002 after the arrest of Ramzi Binalshibh, another of the alleged 9/11 masterminds. Binalshibh had traveled from Quetta to Rawalpindi fearful of being betrayed by the Balochistani Hazars, a group that allegedly collaborated with the CIA in the search for bin Laden in retaliation for the slaughter of Hazars in Afghanistan before 9/11. The Hazars are Shiite Muslims and therefore enemies of the Taliban, who are Sunni Muslim radicals. The slaughter of the Shiites in Quetta on March 2, in turn, was retaliation for their alleged collaboration with the Americans in a search for bin Laden and in part was directed against then President Pervez Musharraf, in order to convince him to soften his measures against the Islamic extremist groups as well as to undermine support for the U.S.

None of this is given any play in the mainstream press. Hundreds of thousands of pages on Pakistan and not a word on the Sunni-Shiite divide? How real is that?

Even before the Iraq invasion, bin Laden's terrorist elements began assembling there from Saudi Arabia and Iran in order to launch a jihad against the Americans. The first group to arrive was the Harkat-ul-Mujahideen (HUM), a terrorist organization very active in Jammu and Kashmir (JYC) and whose center of operations is located in Muzaffarabad, the part of Kashmir occupied by Pakistan, whose sole purpose was to cut off JYC and integrate it with Pakistan. They went as Haj pilgrims to Mecca and from there moved to Iraq. Then, the LEJ, along with Arabic-speaking volunteers of the Lashkar-e-Taiba (LET), the armed wing of the religious organization based in Pakistan, Markaz-ud-Dawawal-Irshad (MDI) – a Sunni missionary anti-American organization founded in 1989 – also began going clandestinely into Iraq. They, in turn, were followed by a large contingent of Jordanian and Saudi Arabs of Chechen origin from South Waziristan, Federally Administered Tribal Areas (FATA).

These tribal areas, or agencies, as they are sometimes called, were created by the British to serve as a buffer zone between India and Afghanistan. "Of those who went to Iraq from Pakistan, only members of the LEJ had previously participated in the massacres of Shiites in Pakistan and Afghanistan and it was expected to participate willingly in similar massacres in Iraq. It is unlikely that the Iraqi resistance was involved in massacres like those carried out in Karbala and Baghdad. According to India's intelligence services, all point to LEJ as a leading suspect. Their position of targeting Shiites in Iraq is due in part to their deep hatred of the Shiites and partly in retaliation for the alleged collaboration of Shiite leaders in Iraq with American troops. Thus, if Iran wanted to provoke clashes between Shiites and Sunnis, with the aim of inciting a civil war in Iraq, as reported by the United States, they would use LEJ, with whom they have had a long history of collaboration and who would not hesitate to kill Shiites, as an ideal execution arm."[19]

However, this hasn't been the case, something that the *New York Times*, *der Spiegel*, the *Guardian* and the *Economist* have chosen to ignore, while focusing their artillery on demonizing Iran and Pakistan.

WikiLeaks, Iran and the ArabWorld

The released WikiLeaks cables are also being used to create divisions between Iran, viewed as a threat to global security by the State Department, Saudi Arabia and the Gulf States: "After WikiLeaks claimed that certain Arab states are concerned about Iran's nuclear program and have urged the U.S. to take [military] action to contain Iran, U.S. Secretary of State Hillary Clinton took advantage of the issue and said that the released cables showed U.S. concerns regarding Iran's nuclear program are shared by the international community."[20]

It should come as no surprise that the *New York Times*, partners in the WikiLeaks project, "steps center stage in its unbridled contempt for truth and relentless use of propaganda to serve U.S. imperial interests,"[21] The *Times* was used to redact and filter the documents, by centring their attention on a highly "selective" dissemination of the WikiLeaks cables.

How does it all fit into the bigger picture?

Michel Chossudovsky of globalresearch.ca explains: "Focussing on areas which would justify a US foreign policy agenda: Iran's alleged nuclear weapons program, North Korea, Saudi Arabia and Pakistan's support of Islamic terrorism, China's relations with North Korea, etc. These releases were then used as source material in NYT articles and commentary" [22] by David E. Sanger and his colleagues "to feed the disinformation campaign."[23]

David E. Sanger, Chief Washington correspondent of the *New York Times*, candidly acknowledges this 'redacting' of the documents:

> [W]e went through [the cables] so carefully to try to redact material that we thought could be damaging to individuals or undercut ongoing operations. And we even took the very unusual step of showing the 100 cables or so that we were writing from to the U.S. government and asking them if they had additional redactions to suggest.[24]

Who exactly is David E. Sanger? For starters, he is a member of the Council on Foreign Relations (CFR) and the Aspen Institute's Strategy Group[25] which includes the likes of David Rockefeller, former Vice President of the United States Dick Cheney, former CIA head John Deutch, the president of the World Bank, Robert B. Zoellick and Henry Kissinger, not to mention every president of the United States except George W. Bush and every director of the Central Intelligence Agency.

The WikiLeaks documents focus on how Iran was fomenting a number of insurgencies in Afghanistan along their border. Fox News ran an article proclaiming that, "Leaked Documents Show Middle East Consensus on Threat Posed by Iran," and commented that, "the seismic document spill by WikiLeaks showed one area of profound agreement – that Iran is viewed in the Middle East as the region's No. 1 troublemaker."[26]

We are left with the meme that we should de-emphasize and downplay the Afghan war and look at our real enemies in the area, the two big states, which are Iran and Pakistan. One of the obvious methods, is to play one off against the other and this is the pattern we are seeing. The US strategy in the entire Middle East is to line up a group of states, which will be Arab and Sunni, against Iran, which is Shi'a. Middle Eastern states like Saudi Arabia and United Arab Emirates are egged on by the United States to attack Iran, because it threatens them. That too, must be understood in terms of local and regional conflicts as described earlier.

In his well researched article "WikiLeaks and the Worldwide Information War," Andrew Gavin Marshall argues that on the one hand, geopolitical alliances and the seeking of favors from the United States have more to do with region-wide condemnation of Iran than anything else. And on the other hand, the leaks are being used to justify a foreign policy agenda:

> Iran is Saudi Arabia's primary contender and competition for power and influence in the region, and thus Iran is, inherently, a threat to Saudi Arabia, politically. Further, the Arab states, whose claims against Iran have been widely publicized, such as those of Saudi Arabia, Bahrain, Oman, the UAE and Egypt, must be understood in their relation to the United States. The Arab states are American proxies in the region. Their armies are subsidized by the American military industrial complex, their political regimes (all of which are dictatorships and dynasties), are propped up and supported by America. The same goes for Israel, although it has at least the public outward appearance of a democracy, much like the United States, itself.
>
> The Arab nations and leaders know that the only reason they have and maintain their power is because the United States allows them and helps them to do so. Thus, they are dependent upon America and its political, financial and military support. Going against America's ambitions in the region is a sure way to end up like Iraq and Saddam Hussein. The history of the Middle East in the modern era is replete with examples of how one-time

119

puppets and personal favorites of the American Empire can so easily turn into new enemies and 'threats to peace.' American sponsored regime change takes place, and a new puppet is installed. If Arab leaders said that Iran was not a threat to peace, they would soon find themselves targets of Western imperialism.[27]

None of these candid analyses or critiques comes through in any of the embassy cables touted by WikiLeaks as the motherload of truth. "Craig Murray was a former British Ambassador to Uzbekistan who made a name for himself in exposing intelligence from Uzbekistan related to al-Qaeda as entirely unreliable, due to the methods of torture used to get the information (such as boiling people alive). This intelligence was passed to the CIA and MI6, which Murray said was 'factually incorrect.' When Murray expressed his concerns with the higher-ups in the British diplomatic services, he was reprimanded for talking about 'human rights.'

In the midst of the latest WikiLeaks releases of diplomatic documents, Craig Murray was asked to write an article for the *Guardian* regarding his interpretation of the issue. As Murray later noted, the paper placed his article, largely reduced, hidden in the middle of a long article which was a compendium of various commentaries on WikiLeaks... In the article, Murray begins by assessing the claims of government officials around the world, particularly in the United States, that WikiLeaks exposes the United States to 'harm,' that it puts lives at risk, and that they will 'encourage Islamic extremism,' and most especially, the notion that 'government secrecy is essential to keep us all safe.' Murray explains that having been a diplomat for over 20 years, he is very familiar with these arguments, particularly that as a result of WikiLeaks, diplomats will no longer be candid in giving advice, 'if that advice might become public....'

Murray pointedly asked why a type of behavior that is considered reprehensible for most people – such as lying – 'should be considered acceptable, or even praiseworthy, in diplomacy.' Murray explained that for British diplomats, 'this belief that their profession exempts them from the normal constraints of decent behavior amounts to a cult of Machiavellianism, a pride in their own amorality.' He explained that diplomats come from a very narrow upper social strata, and 'view themselves as ultra-intelligent Nietzschean supermen, above normal morality' who are socially connected to the political elite. In criticizing the claims made by many commentators that the release of the leaks endanger lives, Murray pointedly wrote that this perspective needs to be 'set against any such risk the hundreds of thousands of actual dead from the foreign policies of the US and its co-conspirators in the past decade.'[28]

Iran's Nuclear Program

The prejudice against Iran is obvious when the mainstream corporate press uses the leaked cables as 'proof' that Iran constitutes a threat, while promulgating its own lies and fabrications concerning Iran's supposed nuclear weapons program on the other. "The leaks, once they are funneled into the corporate news chain, edited and redacted by the New York Times, indelibly serve the broader interests of US foreign policy, including US-NATO-Israel war preparations directed against Iran."[29]

For example, "what are the odds that the first 1,270 cables out of some 251,000 that the *New York Times*, the *Guardian* and *Der Spiegel* published were all in sync with US-UK-Germany-Nato policy outlook? And what are the odds that almost half of the stories initially generated by the three publications focused on Pakistan, its nukes, and its role in Afghanistan, all US top priorities?"[30] – asks well-respected Pakistani journalist Ahmed Quraishi in his scathing critique of information manipulation. He then proceeds to answer the question himself. "This is a propaganda war, not a war for truth, at least not if you go by the initial manipulated stories released by the three news publications."[31]

The manipulation doesn't stop. Chossudovsky unmasks some of the leading players. "With regard to 'leaked intelligence' and the coverage of Iran's alleged nuclear weapons program, David E. Sanger has played a crucial role. In November 2005, The New York Times published a report co-authored by David E. Sanger and William J. Broad entitled "Relying on Computer, U.S. Seeks to Prove Iran's Nuclear Aims."

> The article refers to mysterious documents on a stolen Iranian laptop computer which included 'a series of drawings of a missile re-entry vehicle' which allegedly could accommodate an Iranian produced nuclear weapon.
>
> They [Americans] presented the documents as the strongest evidence yet that, despite Iran's insistence that its nuclear program is peaceful," the country is trying to develop a compact warhead to fit atop its Shahab missile, which can reach Israel and other countries in the Middle East.
>
> These 'secret documents' were "subsequently submitted by the US State Department to the International Atomic Energy Agency IAEA, with a view to demonstrating that Iran was developing a nuclear weapons program. They were also used as a pretext to enforce the economic sanctions regime directed against Iran, adopted by the UN Security Council.[32]

The whole thing blew up in America's face when an article by investigative reporter Gareth Porter confirmed that the mysterious laptop documents are fake.[33] "The drawings contained in the documents leaked by William J. Broad and David E. Sanger pertain to an obsolete North Korean missile system which was decommissioned by Iran in the mid-1990s."[34]

Did the WikiLeaks partners *New York Times*, the *Guardian* of London, *der Spiegel* or *The Economist* print a retraction on the issue of fake intelligence? Not a word. Zero mainstream media coverage. The entire episode was swept under the carpet and forgotten.

Moreover, in a bitter irony, the selective redacting of the WikiLeaks embassy cables by the New York Times has usefully served not only to dismiss the central issue of fake intelligence but also to reinforce, through media disinformation, Washington's claim that Iran is developing nuclear weapons. A case in point is a November 2010 [New York Times] article co-authored by David E. Sanger, which quotes the WikiLeaks cables" as a source: 'Iran obtained 19 of the missiles from North Korea, according to a [WikiLeaks] cable dated Feb. 24 of this year....[35]

Thus, WikiLeaks and Julian Assange fulfill the conditions for a limited-hang-out operation by the intelligence agencies themselves, if we include things like *Project Democracy* on the U.S. side, Soros, the group of foundations which is a part of the intelligence community and a well orchestrated media disinformation campaign aimed at demonizing a powerful regional enemy, Iran.

PRINCES, PLANES AND PAY-OFFS

There is another way in which intelligence agencies across the world use the limited-hang-out operations to cover up blatant usurpation of power. "For example, within the WikiLeaks cables, take the British Prince Andrew, Queen Elizabeth's second son, who has been subject to many cable 'revelations.' The U.S. Ambassador to Kyrgyzstan" wrote a cable regarding a meeting she attended with … Prince Andrew, who is a special U.K. trade representative…. At the meeting, Prince Andrew ranted against 'those [expletive] journalists … who poke their noses everywhere,' and he 'railed at British anticorruption investigators, who had the idiocy of almost scuttling the al-Yamamah deal with Saudi Arabia,' particularly 'referencing an investigation, subsequently closed, into alleged kickbacks a senior Saudi royal had received in exchange for the multi-year, lucrative BAE Systems contract to provide equipment and training to Saudi security forces.' When he ranted against the media – specifically the Guardian paper – for making it harder to do business abroad, the U.S. Ambassador noted that the businessmen in attendance 'roared their approval' and 'practically clapped.' Again, evidence for how elites despise true representations of democracy and freedom."[36] There is a more sinister side to this, which intelligence professionals recognize as bait-and-switch trick.

Accordingly, "Andrew Feinstein, an anti-corruption campaigner and former South African MP who resigned in protest over BAE bribery allegations, said: 'I am amazed but not entirely surprised by the prince's comments. *The royal family has actively supported Britain's arms sales, even when corruption and malfeasance has been suspected.*"[37] [emphasis added]

Furthermore, the *Guardian* would know about the al-Yamamah deal with Saudi Arabia, as they were involved in a decade-long probe "along with the BBC, and the British Serious Fraud Office (SFO), into the al-Yamamah arms contract, a nearly $80 billion, 22-year long deal between BAE Systems and the Saudi government, in which British-made fighter jets and support services were provided to the Saudi Kingdom, beginning in 1985" in return for Saudi delivery of oil to Britain. The deal included an "estimated $2 billion in cumulative payoffs to Prince Bandar," for his role in brokering the al-Yamamah deal. Bandar was the Saudi's "de facto chief diplomat to Britain, the Soviet Union, and China, as well as the U.S.A.," [38]

As Jeffrey Steinberg revealed in the pages of *Executive Intelligence Review*, "every British government, from Margaret Thatcher, through John Major, to Tony Blair, has been thoroughly implicated in the BAE-Saudi scandal."[39] In the intelligence world, this is the 'bait' part of the operation. In other words, people are generally familiar with certain details of the deal as per the mainstream press revelations.

> And here is where the story gets really interesting. Saudi Arabia agreed to provide Britain with one tanker of oil per day, for the entire life of the al-Yamamah contracts.

An oil tanker holds approximately 600,000 barrels of oil. BAE Systems began 'official' delivery of the Tornado and Hawk planes to Saudi Arabia in 1989.... *EIR* economist John Hoefle ... concluded that the total value of the oil sales, based on the value of the dollar at the time of delivery, was $125 billion.

Based on the best available public records, the total sticker price on the military equipment and services provided by BAE Systems to Saudi Arabia, over the 22-year period to date, was approximately $80 billion. And those figures are inflated by billions of dollars in slush fund payouts. Indeed, the latest limited-damage scandal around al-Yamamah erupted in November 2006, when a Ministry of Defence document leaked out, providing the actual sticker price on the fighter jets. The figure confirmed the long-held suspicion that the prices of the jets had been jacked up by at least 40%.

BAE Systems, a crown jewel in the City of London financial/industrial structure, secured somewhere in the range of $80 billion in net profit from the arrangement— in league with BP and Royal Dutch Shell! Where did that money go, and what kinds of activities were financed with it? The answer to those questions, sources emphasize, holds the key to the power of Anglo-Dutch finance in the world today.[40]

In other words, "al-Yamamah is the biggest pool of clandestine cash in history—protected by Her Majesty's Official Secrets Act and the even more impenetrable finances of the City of London and the offshore, unregulated financial havens under British dominion."[41]

This is the "switch" part of the deal. You divert the public's attention long enough with something old, in order to trick them into missing sensationalist revelations that could bring down the government and severely embarrass the Royal family.

According to Steinberg, "At this moment, there is no way of calculating how much of that slush fund has been devoted to the clandestine wars and Anglo-American covert operations of the past two decades. Nor is it possible to estimate the multiplier effect of portions of those undisclosed, and unregulated funds having passed through the hedge funds of the Cayman Island, the Isle of Man, Gibraltar, Panama, and Switzerland.

> What is clear, is that the BAE Systems scandal goes far beyond the $2 billion that allegedly found its way into the pockets of Prince Bandar. It is a scandal that goes to the heart of the power of Anglo-Dutch finance as part of the swindle of the century.[42]

Therefore, in the case of Al-Yamamah, both the *Guardian* and WikiLeaks have served as useful agents of change, obfuscating in the process the real crime behind the less ominous public loss of face.

WAR ON DRUGS

In the spring of 2010, WikiLeaks published hundreds of thousands of pages of allegedly sensitive material from American sources within the Taliban in Afghanistan, showing their links with senior members of the Pakistani intelligence services, not to mention a large quantity of diplomatic cables from U.S. officials revealing 'geopolitical tensions', some relevant and some merely entertaining.

> The evidence suggests however that far from an honest leak, it is a calculated disinformation to the gain of the US and perhaps Israeli and Indian intelligence and a coverup of the US and Western role in drug trafficking out of Afghanistan.[43]

What does drug trafficking, Afghanistan and WikiLeaks have in common? As investigative journalist and economist, William F. Engdahl writes,

> General Hamid Gul, former head of the Pakistani military intelligence agency, ISI, is the man who during the 1980's coordinated the CIA-financed Mujahideen guerilla war in

Afghanistan against the Soviet regime there.... According to London's *Financial Times*, Gul's name appeared "in about 10 of roughly 180 classified US files that allege that Pakistan's intelligence service supported militants in Afghanistan fighting NATO forces. Gul told the newspaper [*Financial Times*] that the U.S. has lost the war in Afghanistan, and that the leak of the documents would help the Obama administration to deflect blame by suggesting that Pakistan was responsible for the defeat....

Conveniently, as if on cue, British Conservative Prime Minister David Cameron, on a state visit to India, lashed out at the alleged role of Pakistan in supporting Taliban in Afghanistan, conveniently lending further credibility to the WikiLeaks story."[44] So, WikiLeaks fits into this agitation just at the proper moment. You can also call these, confirmations and even vindication, depending on which side of the divide you are on.

As well, in a UPI interview on September 26, 2001, two weeks after the 9/11 attacks, Gul stated, in reply to the question who did Black Sept. 11?, 'Mossad and its accomplices. The US spends $40 billion a year on its 11 intelligence agencies. That's $400 billion in 10 years. Yet the Bush Administration says it was taken by surprise. I don't believe it. Within 10 minutes of the second twin tower being hit in the World Trade Center CNN said Osama bin Laden had done it. That was a planned piece of disinformation by the real perpetrators...' Gul is clearly not well liked in Washington. He claims his request for travel visas to the UK and to the USA have repeatedly been denied. Making Gul into the archenemy would suit some in Washington nicely....

The naming of Gul today as a key liaison to the Afghan 'Taliban' forms part of a larger pattern of US and British recent efforts to demonize the current Pakistan regime as a key part of the problems in Afghanistan. Such a demonization greatly boosts the position of recent US military ally, India. Furthermore, Pakistan is the only Muslim country possessing atomic weapons. The Israeli Defense Forces and the Israeli Mossad intelligence agency reportedly would very much like to change that. A phony campaign against the politically outspoken Gul via WikiLeaks could be part of that geopolitical effort.[45]

Gul also has had the temerity to expose the US Army's dirty laundry, as well as its role in the sale of Afghan heroin through the secret American airbase in Manas, Kyrgyzstan.

Is there anything in the WikiLeaks documents on the U.S. military's role in the booming Afghani drug trade? Not a word. Almost a million pages of WikiLeaks documents and not one word on the nefarious drug trade. How is that for a parallel universe of smoke and mirrors? It is beyond doubt that the United States army is in the spotlight for helping the Afghani warlords in transporting opium and heroin. What's more, the CIA and the Pentagon are embroiled in a war of words, with each side accusing the other of controlling the drug trade in Afghanistan.

More than 100 categories dealing with Afghanistan and nothing on America's role in the Afghani drug trade. In a nutshell, "by refusing to go after the opium trade, which is the logistical and financial backbone of the Taliban insurgency, the Obama policy is giving these narco-insurgents a free hand to kill American soldiers."[46]

> President Obama's personal complicity in the opium treachery was demonstrated on March 28, 2010, when he made a 24-hour unannounced visit to Kabul, to scold Afghan President Karzai for his government's corruption, but never mentioned the heroine and opium trade, which accounts for 90% of the world's supply, and bankrolls the very Taliban insurgency that the US Administration purports to be combating.[47]

Needless to say, Obama's visit made the news wires and its records appear in the WikiLeaks. Yet, we are led to believe by the mainstream press that the Pentagon/US Army drug trade connection is the exclusive domain of conspiracy theorists. In stark contrast to what the *New York Times*-WikiLeaks duopoly want us to believe about Obama's policy in Afghanistan,

... the Russian government has called upon the United States and NATO to collaborate on a full-scale war on the Afghan opium and heroin trade, which is the backbone of a global narco-insurgency, now running wild in Eurasia and the Americas, and which has been the cause of at least 1 million drug deaths from Afghan heroin overdoses over the past decade alone, according to United Nations data....

Victor Ivanov, the head of the Russian federal anti-narcotics agency ... cited UN statistics, showing that the Afghan opium trade generated at least $65 billion a year in criminal revenue, and was the principal source of funding for the Taliban insurgency....[48]

What's worse, "under the U.S. occupancy, the Afghan opium business skyrocketed to the point that, as of 2007, Afghanistan was producing 95% of the world's opium and heroin.... To be sure, the U.S. government's policy for de facto support for the Afghan opium apparatus did not begin with the current occupant of the White House. Successive U.S. administrations, going back to 1979,"[49] ... have played a part in it. Jimmy Carter, Ronald Reagan, George H.W. Bush, Clinton, George W. Bush and now Obama. After more than thirty years of U.S. supported drug trade in the region, not a hint of it in the WikiLeaks documents.

"The United States Institute for Peace, a Congressionally established and publicly funded research agency, published a 36-page dossier, 'How Opium Profits the Taliban,' ... which spelled out how the Taliban had evolved into a narcotics cartel.... The insurgency is now synonymous with the narcotics trade."[50] Yes, if we are to believe the heavily redacted Wikileaks reports, the Taliban get the bulk of their funding through Saudi Arabia and Pakistan. Right, and I am a cucumber.

Out of 90,000 pages of documents released by WikiLeaks dated from between 2004 and January 2010, and divided into more than 100 categories, covering much of what the public already knows about the troubled nine-year conflict, not one single word on the drug trade.

CONNECTING DRUGS, MONEY LAUN-DERING AND BIG-TIME BANKING

With the latest release of tens of thousands of pages of banking records and money laundering reports from the world's largest financial institutions, notable for its absence is the complete silence on the ways and means of the international drug trade, supported entirely top down by the world's most powerful banking cartels and governments. Does WikiLeaks mention the reprehensible drug trade and its undeniably close links to the United States government? Not a word. Could they be a part of "over 1.1 million documents"[51] WikiLeaks received in 2006 but has yet to release to the public?

As I explain in, *Shadow Masters*, according to a US Congressional Investigation conducted in 2001, "US and European banks launder between $500 billion and $1 trillion of international criminal proceeds each year, half of which is laundered by US banks alone. It is estimated that half of that money comes to the United States," claims Michigan Senator Carl Levin. In other words, during the 1990s, between $2.5 and $5 trillion (criminal and corrupt money) had been laundered by US banks and circulated in the US financial system. According to informed observers, we can easily double this number today. What does it all mean? Without its illegal money, the US economy would collapse onto itself.

That $250 and $500 billion per year of dirty money covers part of the US deficit in its balance of trade. "Without the 'dirty money,'" stated James Petras, a professor at Binghamton University, "the US economy external accounts would be totally unsustainable, living standards would plummet, the dollar would weaken, the available investment and loan capital would shrink, and Washington would not be able to sustain its global empire."[52]

With mainstream publications such as the *Times*, *Guardian* and *der Spiegel* being the arbiters of the truth, can we expect the real story to be told? I am not suggesting that these scions of the establishment media have hidden the information. They might not have access to it. However, if, as per Julian Assange correspondence, "WikiLeaks is an uncensorable version of wikipedia for untraceable mass document leaking and analysis,"[53] the chances of such vital information not finding its way eventually into Assange's hands is simply beyond belief. In another exchange, Assange stated candidly that "Our overarching goal is to provide a forum where embarrassing information can expose injustice."[54] Would government drug-money laundering qualify as embarrassing information? I surely hope so.

To restate the argument once more: "The *New York Times*, which employs members of the Council on Foreign Relations (CFR) including WikiLeaks' collaborator David E. Sanger, has proven more than once to be a propaganda tool for the US government."[55] With the *New York Times* (Bilderberg, CFR), the *Guardian* (the left wing of the British intelligence agencies), *Der Spiegel* (Bilderberg), The London *Economist* (Bilderberg), "WikiLeaks has enlisted the architects of media disinformation to fight media disinformation: An incongruous and self-defeating procedure,"[56] especially in light of past media transgressions.

We are led to believe that money-laundering is the exclusive domain of Russian Mafiosi and their Italian and Colombian cousins plus a small group of unscrupulous Wall Street bankers. Far from it. Intimately involved in the money-laundering business are the most important banks in the US, sustaining America's global power through management of illegally obtained overseas funds. Again quoting James Petras, "Washington and the mass media have portrayed the US as being in the forefront of the struggle against narco trafficking, drug laundering and political corruption: the image is of clean white hands fighting dirty money. The truth is exactly the opposite. US banks have developed a highly elaborate set of policies for transferring illicit funds to the US, investing those funds in legitimate businesses or US government bonds and legitimizing them."

Do we get a sense of any of this through the latest batch of WikiLeaks reports? No. If WikiLeaks was a real operation and not a part of the government psy-ops, we would have been told what I clearly explain in *Shadow Masters*:

> There are two methods that premier banking institutions use to launder money: through private banks and through correspondent banking. Private banking caters to extremely wealthy clients, requiring minimum deposits of $1 million. Private banks are very attractive for money laundering because more than financial advice, they sell confidentiality to dirty-money clients. Private banks routinely use code names for accounts, establish "concentration accounts" which co-mingle bank funds with client funds (cutting off paper trails for billions of dollars of wire transfers), and set up offshore private investment corporations (PICs) in countries with strict secrecy laws, such as the Cayman Islands, the Bahamas, etc.

"The second route that the big banks use to launder hundreds of billions of dirty money, 'correspondent banking' is a financial technique wherein illicit money is moved from bank to bank with 'no questions asked,' thereby cleansing funds prior to being used for legitimate purposes. In correspondent banking, one bank simply provides services to another in moving funds, exchanging currencies or carrying out other financial transactions. Since this is what banks do, why would a bank incur additional cost by hiring another to do the work?" WikiLeaks would surely know this. Then, why are we not seeing any of it in print?

According to US Congressional hearings, these accounts "give the owners and clients of poorly regulated, poorly managed, sometimes corrupt foreign banks, with weak or no anti-money laundering controls, direct access to the US financial system and the freedom to move money within the United States and around the world."[57] Needless to say, some of these customers would include drug dealers and others engaged in criminal activity. Some of the biggest banks specializing in international-fund transfer process up to $1 trillion in wire transfers per day.[58]

Would WikiLeaks have access to this information? Of course they would. After all, money is laundered through the world's biggest banks, whose paper and electronic trail WikiLeaks has allegedly been exposing. Or have they? It is imperative to explain the whole nefarious business of drugs, to show just how improbable it would have been for WikiLeaks to miss the signs.

A Short History of Drugs

Let's start by saying that drug money is an inherent part of the American and world economy. In following global cash flows, it's staggering to find that the amount of profit generated annually by the drug trade is somewhere around $900 billion. This figure includes heroin, opium, morphine, marijuana, cocaine, crack cocaine and hallucinogens. As noted, drug money is now "an essential part of the world banking and financial system because it provides the liquid cash necessary to make the 'minimum monthly payments' on huge stock and derivative and investment bubbles in the US and Britain."[59]

How can $900 billion in illegal profits criss-crossing international borders get through the international banking system and past the eyes and ears of law enforcement authorities? The answer takes us behind the corporate board rooms and precious metal exchanges to the inner sanctum of some of the world's wealthiest people: eight to ten generations of men who built their empires around the opium trade. This may seem more like fiction than fact. But fact it is recorded in the available documents at the National Library of Singapore, the National Archives of India, the University of London, the British Library, the Jardine Matheson Archives at the University of Cambridge Library, and the British East Indian Company Archives, as well as government records in Hong Kong and Macao. It began in the seventeenth century and involved a long succession of empire builders. This included Robert Clive and Warren Hastings in the eighteenth century, and Alexander Matheson, David Sasoon, the Perkins and the Codmans, the Russells and the Appletons, the Boylestons and the Cunninghams amongst a plethora of others in the nineteenth. Opium represented fantastic gobs of money beyond anyone's wildest dreams. Nobody needed to remind these men that money made the world go around. They were empire builders in the corridors of power, and filthy drug runners from the underbelly of history.

We are talking about the most highly organized, top-down political machinery in the world, enjoying the logistical support of a $900-billion-per-annum international cartel, and the protection of every political entity that Britain and the US have created through these vast invisible earnings. This protection applies not merely to growing and distribution, but to providing political, intelligence, and ideological support as well. Like international terrorism, it just can't quite ever be stamped out: indicating that some of the biggest names in royal circles and the international oligarchy/plutocracy are the puppeteers, who manage through cut outs and intermediaries, concealing the identities of those pulling the strings.

Nor should we forget the gigantic support facilities of the world's official credit markets, the gold and diamond trade, and "hands-on" management of retail distribution, through organized crime. They are all derivatives of Drugs Incorporated. One purpose of the drug trade is to create unseen liquid capital, and to make it available to those wishing to gain an unfair advantage in the marketplace. This cash must go through nominally legitimate channels, in such mind-boggling volumes that the banks and other financial institutions cannot possibly be unaware of the origin of the funds. The fact that most of this money flow is seasonal, completed during the two months following the March poppy harvest, can only add to our stupor. Banks pleading ignorance – "We didn't know" – is simply absurd.

The 900 billion dollars a year in illegal drug money benefits financial markets and especially Wall Street. That's the reason for maintaining the illegal drug trade. *From The Wilderness* Contributing Editor Catherine Austin Fitts, George H.W. Bush's Assistant Secretary of Housing, and a former managing director at Dillon Read with ample experience as a Wall Street investment banker, has been a crusader in the effort to expose the underbelly. She and her new investment firm were quickly targeted for investigation by both the Department of Justice and HUD. This experience is described in some detail in her 13-part Internet article "Narco-Dollars For Beginners: How The Money Works In The Illicit Drug Trade." The following excerpts are from that highly recommended piece, which looks at the problem from the bottom up as well as the top down:

"Every day there are two or three teenagers on the corner dealing drugs across from our home in Philadelphia. We figured that if they had a 50% deal with a supplier, did $300 a day of sales each, and worked 250 days a year that their supplier could run his net profits of approximately $100,000 through a local fast food restaurant that was owned by a publicly traded company. Assuming that company has a stock market value that is a multiple of 20-30 times its profits, a handful of illiterate teenagers could generate approximately $2-3 million in stock market value for a major corporation, not to mention a nice flow of deposits and business for the Philadelphia banks and insurance companies....

"So if I have a company that has a $100,000 of income and a stock trading at 20 times earnings, if I can find a way to run $100,000 of narcotics sales by a few teenagers in West Philadelphia through my financial statements, I can get my stock market value to go up from $2 million to $4 million. I can double my "pop." That is a quick $2 million profit from putting a few teenagers to work ... The

135

total stock market value generated in the Philadelphia area with $20-40 billion in narco retail sales would be about $80-160 billion. If you add all the things you could do with debt or and other ways to increase the multiples, and you could get that even higher, say $100-250 billion.... The problems this presents to people trying to run an honest business are numerous. The problems it creates for our work ethic and culture are numerous too. It increasingly puts the low performance people in charge, and everyone starts to behave like and follow them...."[60]

What does this mean in the world of high finance? If firms like Hong Kong and Shanghai Bank, Bank of Nova Scotia, Royal Bank of Scotland, Chase Manhattan Bank, Citibank, or General Electric were to have an additional $40 million in earnings from the drug trade, with a price-to-earnings multiplier of 20, the net increase in their company's equity would be $800 million. If you still believe that there cannot really be major, hands-on, institutional involvement in the drug trade, you will be surprised to hear that in late June 1999, numerous news services, including the Associated Press, reported that Richard A. Grasso, then Chairman of the New York Stock Exchange, flew down to Colombia for a jungle encounter with a spokesperson for Raul Reyes of the Revolutionary Armed Forces of Columbia (FARC). FARC is Colombia's major narco-terrorist outfit, with which the United States government is unofficially at war.

The purpose of the trip was "to bring a message of co-operation from US financial services"[61] and to discuss foreign investment and the future role of US businesses in Colombia. What does Colombia have that the United States could possibly want? Money – drug money: over a trillion dollars in equity that has been building up in Colombia for over thirty years now. These are practically limitless resources that make Wall Street salivate at the thought of channelling them through its financial markets.

What do we get in WikiLeaks? The usual nonsense: The FARC narco-terrorists and their Russian mafia partners effortlessly launder drug money through the world's leading financial institutions without their knowledge. The reality is quite different.

However, before they can channel this money into actual year-end results, something needs to be done to legitimize it. Unlike one hundred and fifty years ago, profits from the lucrative drug trade are illegal. That's another thing often overlooked by people trying to understand how the entire nefarious business of drugs works. Before that money can be used legally, it needs to hide, then be laundered. You can't hide nine hundred billion dollars in a mattress. "The money moves so quickly that, unless one were in control of the computer systems that handle it, or the software that manages it, it would be impossible to trace."[62] Ignorance, therefore, especially when the laundering transactions are gigantic ones, is not a tenable position.

Additionally, corporations can earn a fantastic amount of money by borrowing illegal money from drug dealers and drug-dealing nations at a lower interest rate and laundering it into astronomical profits. When 100 billion dollars of useless illegal money is loaned at five percent to a giant corporation, the money, in turn becomes legal and liquid.

"*Le Monde Diplomatique*, the premier information source for international diplomats, found US intelligence services, banks, and other multinational corporations at the top of a huge global network of organized crime and money laundering.... [It cited] "cartels, insider dealing and speculation, fraudulent balance sheets, embezzlement of public funds, spying, blackmail, and betrayal, among a host of other seamy practices. But these cannot succeed without governments willing to 'keep restrictive regulations to a minimum, to abolish or override such rules as do exist, to paralyse inquiries ... and to reduce or grant amnesty from any penalties.'"[63]

From Vietnam to Cambodia, from Laos to Pakistan and Afghanistan, from Iran to the Contras and beyond, the Central Intelligence Agency has been the progressive left's favorite whipping boy. However, it isn't only the CIA who are up to their eyeballs in drugs. In the aforementioned article, *Le Monde Diplomatique* explicitly stated that "the secret services of the world's most powerful state apparatus ... have moved into economic warfare,"[64] becoming "international financial crime's number-one partner."[65] The same charge can be levelled at the British Foreign Intelligence (MI6), the Israeli Mossad, French DGSE, Russian FSB, not to mention intelligence agencies from Morocco, Colombia, Honduras, El Salvador, Venezuela, Panama, Dominican Republic, the Philippines and beyond.

Christian de Brie and Jean de Maillard, in that brilliant article for *Le Monde Diplomatique's* April 2000 issue, describe a tangible "operating system" of international drug capital flow: "By allowing capital to flow unchecked from one end of the world to the other, globalization and abandon of sovereignty have together fostered the explosive growth of an outlaw financial market. It is a coherent system closely linked to the expansion of modern capitalism and based on an association of three partners: governments, transnational corporations and Mafias.

"Business is business: financial crime is first and foremost a market, thriving and structured, ruled by supply and demand. Big business complicity and political *laisser faire* is the only way that large scale organized crime can launder and recycle the fabulous proceeds of its activities. And the transnationals need the support of governments and the neutrality of regulatory authorities in order to consolidate their positions, increase their profits, withstand and crush the competition, pull off the 'deal of the century' and finance their illicit operations. Politicians are directly involved and their ability to intervene depends on the backing and the funding that keep them in power. This collusion of interests is an essential part of the world economy, the oil that keeps the wheels of capitalism turning."[66]

In other words, drugs are big business, run, controlled and protected by very powerful people who work alongside leading banking institutions on both sides of the Atlantic, members of various governments and principal corporations whose stock is traded on the world's leading stock exchanges. One such institution is the Hong Kong and Shanghai Corporation (BHSH). Out of the second Opium War (1858-60), the British merchant banks and trading companies established BHSH, "which to this day serves as the central clearinghouse for all Far Eastern financial transactions relating to the black market in opium and its heroin derivatives."[67]

Another suspect is Canada's Bank of Nova Scotia, now headquartered in Toronto. On the one hand, it serves as a major gold dealer and leader of the Toronto gold market, and on the other, it serves as banker for giant Canadian mining companies operating in the third world. According to knowledgeable US intelligence sources, the Bank of Nova Scotia may be a major dirty money operator in the Caribbean, running flight-capital against currency restrictions, a serious violation of local currency laws.

"How do banks with their great air of respectability fit into the drug trade with all of its attendant filth?"[68] One way is by financing legitimate purchases of companies registered and licensed to do business as importers of chemicals. The Hong Kong and Shanghai Bank is "right in the middle of such trade through a company called Tejapaibul, which banks with BHSH. What does this company do? It imports into Hong Kong most of the chemicals"[69] needed to process raw opium into heroin by the diacetylation of morphine with acetic anhydride, the irreplaceable chemical agent in heroin processing. Acetic anhydride is also used in the conversion of cellulose into acetate, a component of photographic film, and in the production of aspirin. It should be no surprise, then, that the largest markets for diverted acetic anhydride continue to be in Afghanistan.

Tens of thousands of pages and over 100 categories of blanket coverage of the war in Afghanistan and not one word on the largest markets for diverted acetic anhydride – Afghanistan. Please understand, according to WikiLeaks documents, the drug business, the drug trade, the drug profits and the drug wars all are a figment of overblown, conspiracy-oriented, sick imagination. It does not exist. End of story.

The virtue of patience is rewarded in the business of countering counter-intelligence, the web of deceit employing disinformation called psy-ops to put spin on the reality of facts, which cannot be otherwise concealed. With certain training and identifiable targets, the sniper out to expose liars need only wait for a mistake to be made.

The facts are undeniable. If you eradicate the drug trade, the entire world economy will collapse onto itself. But then, the government knows it, which is why US and Canadian and Spanish and British troops have been occupying Afghanistan for the past decade.

Everyone in the business of war and politics understands it. Everyone, except, apparently, WikiLeaks.

(ENDNOTES)

1   Michel Chossudovsky, "Who is Behind WikiLeaks," globalresearch.ca, December 13, 2010.

2   Nick Davies, "Afghanistan war logs: Story behind biggest leak in intelligence history," Guardian, July 25, 2010.

3   CNN Wire Staff, "Leaked reports describe Afghan war, sometimes in mundane detail," CNN, July 26, 2010.

4   John Hoefle, "The BAE Systems Affair and The Anglo-Dutch Imperial Slime Mold," EIR, July 6, 2007. http://www.larouchepub.com/other/2007/3427bae_slimemold.html.

5   CNN wire staff, "Leaked reports describe Afghan war, sometimes in mundane detail," July 26, 2010.

6   http://en.wikipedia.org/wiki/Cryptome.

7   http://cryptome.org/0002/wl-diary-mirror.htm.

9   Michel Chossudovsky, "Who is behind WikiLeaks?," globalresearch.ca, December 13, 2010.

10   Ibid.

11   Ibid.

12   Arundhati Roy, "War is Peace," Outlook, October 18, 2001. http://coat.ncf.ca/our_magazine/links/issue47/articles/a14.htm.

13   Michel Chossudovsky, "Who is behind WikiLeaks?," globalresearch.ca, December

13, 2010.

14   http://www.outlookindia.com/article.aspx?213547

15   Elizabeth Gould & Paul Fitzgerald, "Thinking outside the box? No! Throw the box away," www.boilingfrogspost.com, October 15, 2010.

16   Andrew Gavin Marshall, "WikiLeaks and the Worldwide Information War," www.globalresearch.ca, December 6, 2010.

17   Arundhati Roy, "War is Peace," *Outlook*, October 18, 2001. http://www.outlookindia.com/full.asp?fodname=20011029&fname=arundhati%20(F)&sid=1.

18   Andrew Gavin Marshall, "WikiLeaks and the Worldwide Information War," globalresearch.ca, December 6, 2010.

19   Ibid.

20   B. Raman, "Pakistan: Bloody Sectarian Legacies," *Kashmir Telegraph*, Vol. 3, #10, March 2004. http://the.kashmirtelegraph.com/0304/four.htm (paraphrased).

21   Ibid.

22   Ibid.

23   "WikiLeaks promoting Iranophobia," *Tehran Times*, December 5, 2010.

24   Andrew Gavin Marshall, "WikiLeaks and the Worldwide Information War," globalresearch.ca, December 6, 2010.

25   Michel Chossudovski, "Who is behind WikiLeaks?," globalresearch.ca, December 13, 2010.

26   Ibid.

27   "The Redacting and Selection of WikiLeaks documents by the Corporate Media," PBS interview on "Fresh Air" with Terry Gross: December 8, 2010. http://www.globalresearch.ca/index.php?context=va&aid=22378.

28   http://www.aspeninstitute.org/policy-work/aspen-strategy-group/about-aspen-strategy-group/group-members.

29   "Leaked Documents Show Middle East Consensus on Threat Posed by Iran," Fox News, 29 November 2010: http://www.foxnews.com/politics/2010/11/29/leaked-documents-middle-east-consensus-threat-posed-iran/

30   Andrew Gavin Marshall, "WikiLeaks and the Worldwide Information War: Power, Propaganda, and the Global Political Awakening," globalresearch.ca, December 13, 2010.

31   Ibid.

32   Michel Chossudovsky, "Who is behind WikiLeaks?" globalresearch.ca, December 13, 2010.

33   "*Guardian* Uses WikiLeaks For Propaganda, Pakistani Media Can't?" Siasat.pk, December 10, 2010. http://www.defence.pk/forums/current-events-social-issues/84078-guardian-uses-wikileaks-propaganda-pakistani-media-can-t.html

34   Ibid.

35   Michel Chossudovsky, "Who is behind WikiLeaks?" globalresearch.ca, December 13, 2010.

36   Gareth Porter, "Exclusive Report: Evidence of Iran Nuclear Weapons Program May Be Fraudulent," Global Research, November 18, 2010.

37   Michel Chossudovsky, "Who is behind WikiLeaks," globalresearch.ca, December 13, 2010.

38   Ibid.

39   Ibid.

40   Rob Evans and David Leigh, "WikiLeaks cables: Prince Andrew demanded special BAE briefing," *Guardian*, 30 November 2010: http://www.guardian.co.uk/uk/2010/nov/30/prince-andrew-wikileaks-cables.

41   Jeffrey Steinberg, "Scandal of the Century Rocks British Crown and the City," EIR, June 22, 2007.

42   Ibid.

43   Ibid.

44   Ibid.

45   Ibid.

46   F. William Engdahl, "Hidden Intelligence Operation Behind the WikiLeaks Release of 'Secret' Documents?" Globalresearch.ca, August 11, 2010.

47   Ibid.

48   F. William Engdahl, "Something Stinks About WikiLeaks," August 03, 2010. http://www.financialsense.com/contributors/william-engdahl/something-stinks-about-wikileaks.

49   Jeffrey Steinberg, "Obama's Afghan Policy Is Tantamount to Treason," EIR, April 9, 2010. http://www.larouchepub.com/other/2010/3714lar_demands_impeach.html.

50   Ibid.

51   Ibid.

52   Ibid.

53   Ibid.

54   Wiki internal mailing list, released through Chrome.org, January 7, 2005.

55   James Petras "'Dirty Money' Foundation of U.S. Growth and Empire, La Jornada, May 19, 2001 http://www.narconews.com/petras1.html

56   Michel Chossudovsky, "Who is behind WikiLeaks?" globalresearch.ca, December 13, 2010.

57   http://Wikileaks.org/wiki/WikiLeaks/pt.

58   by Julie Lévesque, "Who is Who at WikiLeaks," globalresearch.ca, December 20, 2010.

56   Michel Chossudovsky, "Who is Behind WikiLeaks," globalresearch.ca, December 13, 2010.

57   MINORITY STAFF OF THE PERMANENT SUBCOMMITTEE ON INVESTIGATIONS REPORT ON CORRESPONDENT BANKING: A GATEWAY FOR MONEY LAUNDERING, February 5, 2001 http://hsgac.senate.gov/psi_finalreport.pdf.

58   James Petras "'Dirty Money' Foundation of U.S. Growth and Empire, La Jornada, May 19, 2001 http://www.narconews.com/petras1.html.

59   Michael Ruppert, Crossing the Rubicon, New Society Publishers, 2004.

60   Catherine Austin Fitts, "Solari Rising," Philadelphia City Paper, November 15-22, 2001. http://archives.citypaper.net/articles/111501/sl.slant.shtml?print=1.

61   Reuters, "NYSE Chief Meets Top Columbia Rebel Leader," June 26, 1999.

62   Michael Ruppert, Crossing the Rubicon, New Society Publishers, 2004.

63   Ed Ripy, "9-11 and US Global Hegemony, Indymedia, 17 July 2002. http://www.globalresearch.ca/articles/RIP207A.html.

64   Christian de Brie, Think as Thieves, Le Monde Diplomatique, April 5, 2001. Translated by Malcolm Greenwood. http://mondediplo.com/2000/04/05debrie

65   Ibid.

66   Ibid.

67   Konstandinos Kalimtgis also by David Goldman and Jeffrey Steinberg, Dope inc.: Britain's opium war against the U.S, 1978. http://www.whale.to/b/dopeinc.html.

68   Gyeorgos C. Hatonn, Political Psychos, Phoenix Source Publishers, p.36, 1994.

http://books.google.com/books.

69   Ibid.

TIME

Do You Want to Know a Secret?

Why WikiLeaks' Julian Assange has so many of them

BY MASSIMO CALABRESI

And why it hasn't hurt America

BY FAREED ZAKARIA

www.time.c

Chapter 3

WikiLeaks and the
World of Smoke and Mirrors

In the second volume of his magnificent trilogy, *Sinister Forces*, author Peter Levenda writes: "Richard Mellon Scaife, scion of the Mellon fortune and heavy financial backer of the conservative movement in America – including the campaign to discredit and eventually impeach Bill Clinton – made a most revealing remark when he addressed the Heritage Foundation in the heady days of the Republican Party winning control of Congress in the November 1994 election. He said that 'ideological conflicts' had 'swirled about this nation for half a century,' that is since about 1945. Further, he warned that the nation was on the verge of breaking out into 'ideological warfare in which the very foundations of our republic are threatened.' This can not be understood without reference to the last days of the Second World War, and the polarization of the two most powerful American political parties on either side of the right-versus-left conflict, as Nazis were being recruited into the American intelligence, aerospace, medical and scientific establishment as a means of combating the Communist threat.

"Deep into the Clinton presidency, a right-wing ideologue was giving voice to what a generation of conservatives and rightist Republicans feared most: that with the collapse of the Soviet Union and the demonstration that Communism was politically bankrupt, America would not take the initiative and extend its hegemony – even, according to some, its imperialism – over the rest of the world. To the Republicans, the Democrats were throwing away the one best chance America had to bring the entire world to heel....

This was indeed an ideological conflict, and it was supported by powerful and influential people and organizations in the United States, with their ideology exported abroad in the support of vicious dictatorships of every stripe: essential elements of a 'bulwark against Communism....'

Taken together, this was nothing less than a redesign of the American political and religious environment, an attempt to create a new country, one worthy of the mantle of global liberator, a liberator with its eyes on the domination not only of the world, but of space, as well. And, in order to create this new country, this new spiritual paradigm with new rules of engagement and a strange new morality in which some of the most brutal regimes the world has ever known – the Nazis and the Imperial Japanese – would become our allies against 'godless Communists' and the 'yellow peril,' we had to take measures that were harsh and ruthless.

The war against Communism took more out of American society than the war against Nazism. For one thing, it lasted much longer and, as Communism was an "international" enemy and painted as more truly an ideological enemy than Nazism, anyone could be a Communist. Your neighbor, your boss, your employee, your brother, your senator and even—in the eyes of some—your president. America turned inward upon itself in its search for socialists, Communists, "reds" in general and their fellow-travelers. While Eleanor Roosevelt and Albert Einstein and Helen Douglas were in New York City raising consciousness and voice against the importation of war criminals under the Operation Paperclip program, the Dulles brothers and Richard Nixon were plotting an extension of that program to include thousands more. It was an ideological conflict that perhaps had its origins in American history decades if not centuries earlier, but which only became refined and fine-tuned during the war years.[1]

Against the backdrop of frightening conflict in Southeast Asia, with images of American soldiers returning home in flag-draped coffins, America learned that it was secretly wiping out entire villages of Viet Cong collaborators and sympathizers. America learned that the White House operated on quite another level, one of realpolitik, one that did not respect Congress and the laws it had passed. America learned that people in positions of power and influence (non-elected positions) had nothing but disdain and contempt for the elected officials of Congress. But then, what did we expect from a Richard Nixon? And all this in the midst of Vietnam, Laos, Cambodia, African revolutions and Latin American coups d'etat. The real and the ideal were mixed in a kaleidoscopic mural of love, hate and death, hope and despair.

> As Vietnam turned into Watergate, reality itself became the circus of the bizarre. We learned more during the Watergate hearings than we ever wanted to know. Crooked politicians we could deal with, and have dealt with since the founding of the country; but crooked spies, rogue intelligence operations, foreign adventures unsupported by an electorate glued to their television sets during prime time soap opera extravaganzas... this was more than most Americans could understand.[2]

Gradually, entertainment became reality, and reality, entertainment. Not long after that, entertainment became king. Dead men and body bags. With Vietnam, there was an example of a new kind of post-war Romanticism: horror in movies was acceptable if it was real. With the Pentagon Papers and Daniel Ellsberg, we had a new kind of entertainment.

*****

Today we are hearing from Julian Assange that he is the modern day Daniel Ellsberg.
In a January 5, 2007 email, Assange uses the image of Ellsberg to describe his operation:

147

Consider Daniel Ellsberg, working within the US government during the Vietnam War. He comes into contact
with the Pentagon Papers, a meticulously kept record
of military and strategic planning throughout the war.
Those papers reveal the depths to which the US government has sunk in deceiving the population about the war.
Yet the public and the media know nothing of this urgent
and shocking information. Indeed, secrecy laws are being
used to keep the public ignorant of gross dishonesty prac-
tised by their government. In spite of those secrecy laws
and at great personal risk, Ellsberg manages to dissemi-
nate the Pentagon papers to journalists and to the world.
Despite facing criminal charges, eventually dropped, the
release of the Pentagon papers shocks the world, exposes
the government, and helps to shorten the war and save
thousands of lives.[3]

In fact, Assange's earlier admiration for Ellsberg comes
through clearly in the following email, written on December
9, 2006:

Dear Mr. Ellsberg.

We have followed with interest and delight your recent statements on document leaking.

We have come to the conclusion that fomenting a world wide
movement of mass leaking is the most cost effective political
intervention available to us* We believe that injustice is answered by good governance and for there to be good governance there must be open governance. Governance by stealth
is governance by conspiracy and fear. Fear, because without it,
secrecy does not last for long. Retired generals and diplomats
are vociferous, but those in active service hold their tune.

Lord Action said, "Everything secret degenerates, even the administration of justice; nothing is safe that does not show how
it can bear discussion and publicity."

This degeneration comes about because when injustice is
concealed, including plans for future injustice, it cannot be
addressed. When governance is closed, man's eyes become
cataracts. When governance is open, man can see and so act
to move the world towards a more just state; for instance see

http://en.wikipedia.org/wiki/Reporters_Without_Borders which shows a striking correlation between press freedom and countries known for their quality of life.

us*: some attributes may have been swapped to protect selected identities, no particular order.

1) Retired new york architect and notorious intelligence leak facilitator
2) Euro cryptographer/programmer
3) Pacific physicist and illustrator
4) A pacific author and economic policy lecturer
5) Euro, Ex-Cambridge mathematician/cryptographer/programmer
6) Euro businessman and security specialist/activist
7) Author of software than runs 40% of the world's websites.
8) US pure mathematician with criminal law background
9) An infamous US ex-hacker
10) Pacific cryptographer/physicist and activist
11) US/euro cryptographer and activist/programmer
12) Pacific programmer
13) Pacific architect / foreign policy wonk

New technology and cryptographic ideas permit us to not only encourage document leaking, but to facilitate it directly on a mass scale. We intend to place a new star in the political firmament of man.

We are building an uncensorizable branch of Wikipedia for leaked documents and the civic institutions & social perceptions necessary to defend and promote it. We have received over 1 million documents from 13 countries, despite not having publicly launched yet!

We have approached you now for two reasons.

Firstly, we have crossed over from 'prospective' to 'projective'. The basic technology has been prototyped and we have a view as how we must proceed politically and legally. We need to move and inspire people, gain volunteers, funding, further set up the necessary political-legal defences and deploy. Since you have thought about leaking more than anyone we know, we would like you on board. We'd like your advice and we'd like you to form part of our political armour. The more armour we have, particularly in the form of men and women sanctified by age, history and class, the more we can act like brazen young men and get away with it.

Secondly, we would like to award "The Ellsburg Prize for Courageous Action" and "The Ellsburg Prize for Courageous Action (USA)," for the two leaks submitted in the past year which most assist humanity. The regionalization of the second prize is to encourage patrons of similar awards in other countries. Although it is premature to go into detail, we have designed a scheme were this can be meaningfully awarded to anonymous leakers. We have been pledged substantial initial funding.

Please tell us your thoughts. If you are happy, we will add you to our internal mailinglist, contacts, etc.

Solidarity!

WL.[4]

THE PENTAGON PAPERS

In the middle of 1967, Robert S. McNamara, who was then Secretary of Defense, made what turned out to be one of his most important decisions in his seven years at the Pentagon. He commissioned a study that has since became known as the Pentagon Papers – an allegedly "massive top-secret history of the United States role in Indochina. The result was approximately 3,000 pages of narrative history and more than 4,000 pages of appended documents – an estimated total of 2.5 million words. The 47 volumes cover American involvement in Indochina from World War II to May 1968, the month that peace talks began in Paris"[5] after President Johnson had set a limit on further military commitments and revealed his intention to retire. Pentagon Papers "revealed that the United States government had been misrepresenting the facts of the Vietnam War's chances of success."[6]

As the official story goes, Department of Defense employee and one-time hippie, Daniel Ellsberg, allegedly leaked a treasure trove of *Top Secret* papers to the *New York Times* which began publishing a series of articles on June 13, 1971. According to the *Times*, "the papers tell what decisions were made, how and why they were made and who made them.

The story is told in the written words of the principal actors themselves – in their memorandums, their cablegrams an their orders."[7] These, subsequently, were "banned by the Nixon administration, and resumed publishing excerpts two weeks later after the Supreme Court ruled the presidency did not have the right to forbid its publication by the media."[8]

The real story of the Pentagon Papers was quite different. As L. Marcus (Lyndon LaRouche) explains in the April 1974 issue of the *Campaigner* magazine: "The essential thrust of the project was the assembly of selected actual documents (many initially created by the CIA or based on the CIA briefings) and supplementary materials whose overall intended effect was to exonerate the CIA from responsibility for a wide variety of unpopular military and related developments which the CIA itself had chiefly authored. In essence, the effect of the 'Pentagon Papers' was – for anyone credulous enough to believe them – to whitewash the CIA for its own activities."[9]

This is absolutely consistent with methodology using a select collection of authentic documents employed to deceive as described in *The Secret Team*[10] by Colonel Prouty, former Joint Chiefs of Staff/CIA liason. Colonel Prouty pointed out that the Pentagon Papers had been a deliberately engineered psychological operation to shift political responsibility, in the public eye, for the colossal intelligence and policy failures in Vietnam, stating: "This psy-ops trick does not conceal the policy failures, that cannot be done. What is actually happening here is a deliberate twist put on the facts to further the political agenda of one party undermining another party with dirty tricks."[11]

Marcus asks a number of fundamental questions which help us understand the way the operation was put together. "Can it be believed that such an effort was undertaken with the intended purpose of concealing the false report under a 'top secret' seal? The entire concoction is in the fine old tradition of the czarist Okhrana's notorious anti-Semitic pioneering venture into modern 'Black' psychological warfare, the Czarist-authored 'protocols of Zion.' Such 'secret' documents are written for the purpose of affording them the widest possible public attention. The 'top secret' classification is the fine hand of the public relations specialist, who thereby assures himself that his handywork will receive the widest circulation and simultaneously evoke the maximum awe from among the credulous public."[12]

Before touching on the WikiLeaks hoax, I would like to explain how the Pentagon Papers hoax was accomplished. "Would the CIA arrange for its publication in a way which would be directly attributed to its sponsorship? Scarcely! A devious confidence man's procedure was indicated. Through Ellsberg's performance, the desired effect was secured. An outright fraud was hallowed for a gullible public by representing the concoction as 'a most secret document, filched from the most intimate files of the most all-powerful agencies at unspeakable risk by an astonishingly courageous, conscience-striken' ... CIA operative!"[13] That's right. Ellsberg, after all was a lifetime CIA employee.

> As of this date, no secret has been made of the general way in which the so-called 'Pentagon Papers' were 'compiled.' Firstly, "the papers were not compiled by or for the 'Pentagon,' but on behalf of the CIA, with complicity of such CIA adjuncts as the RAND Corporation, with the selection and supplementary concoction of included documents.[14]

RAND is a non-profit organization created to connect military planning with research and development decisions.[15] RAND has also been referred to as the U.S. Brainwashing Institute, for its experiments in methodology for social planning and psychological response to stress.

Ellsberg, who inexplicably remains a hero and a 'patriot' to most leftists, was a nuclear weapons planner from the RAND Corporation, as well as a member of Henry Kissinger's staff at the White House. We were told that he had a Damascus Road conversion, became antiwar and, allegedly in an effort to stop the war, released documents.

Marcus places the blame for making the Pentagon Papers hoax possible on one of the more beloved 'left wing' intellectuals, MIT Professor Noam Chomsky. Marcus states: "the manner in which the desired leak was effected is only less 'hairy' than the papers themselves. To explain how and why a right wing CIA operative, Ellsberg, an associate of general Ed Lansdale, could be converted, the public has been told that the convenient 'Damascus Road' transformation was accomplished under the influence of Professor Noam Chomsky of MIT, an individual with a credible standing as a leading anti war activist. Chomsky's role as the official dupe in the affair grows murky when we note Chomsky's endorsement of the hoax after its publication. As a leading anti-war activist, Chomsky had abundant access to all the knowledge necessary to spot the whitewashing of the CIA as a blatant fraud."[16]

In the same way and under the same guise, Chomsky has steadfastly refused to acknowledge U.S. government complicity in the September 11, 2001 attacks.

> General" Edward Lansdale was a CIA man and Deputy Assistant Secretary of the Pentagon's Office of Special Operations at the time of the planning of the Bay of Pigs. He was the head of the top secret intelligence project known as 'Operation Mongoose,' "drawn up after President John F. Kennedy had shifted responsibility for dealing with Cuba, in late 1961, from the CIA to the Department of Defense (DOD), in the aftermath of the Bay of Pigs. ... According to documents that were intended to have been destroyed almost 40 years ago, top levels of the U.S. military proposed carrying out acts of terrorism against the United States in the early 1960s, in order to drag the United States into a war against Cuba.[17]

What does this have to do with WikiLeaks? A great deal, as shall become clear shortly.

The publication effected through the usual CIA press conduits, the New York Times et al., a Rockefeller CIA operative, Henry Kissinger, allegedly ordered the CIA unit from the White House basement to investigate Ellsberg ... beginning to set up an even bigger CIA hoax.[18]

The actual background of the 'coming out party' for WikiLeaks sounds just as improbable as the now-revealed Pentagon Papers hoax and the Watergate hoax, which ousted U.S. President, Richard Nixon. "A closer look at the details, so far carefully leaked by the most ultra-establishment of international media such as the *New York Times*, reveals a clear agenda. That agenda coincidentally serves to buttress the agenda of US geopolitics around the world from Iran to Russia to North Korea and Pakistan."[19]

"Now, we have a cyber-age repeat of the 'Pentagon Papers.' What did the 'Pentagon Papers' episode serve to do?"[20] As Colonel Prouty pointed out in *The Secret Team*, the Pentagon Papers are "unreliable, inaccurate and marred by serious omissions. They are a contrived history"[21]

"A professionally engineered psychological operation, it shifted, for the public consumption, responsibility for the colossal intelligence and policy failures in Vietnam, from the CIA to the military."[22] In the end, only the CIA and their close friends in the military/industrial complex who profit from war, and those promoted CIA agents in military service cover, benefited. Accountability never happened. Now, with Afghanistan becoming a colossal political and military failure, the 'goal posts' have been moved again, changing the direction of the emphasis from Afghanistan to the two regional powerhouses, Iran and Pakistan.

Assange may well be the modern day Daniel Ellsberg. His story, in fact, might well have been written by the people behind the Pentagon Papers hoax. As F. William Engdahl writes,

The story on the surface makes for a script for a new Oliver Stone Hollywood thriller. A 39-year old Australian hacker holds the President of the United States and his State Department hostage to a gigantic cyber 'leak,' unless the President leaves Julian Assange and his WikiLeaks free to release hundreds of thousands of pages of sensitive US Government memos....

It is almost too perfectly-scripted to be true. A discontented 22-year old US Army soldier on duty in Baghdad, Bradley Manning, a low-grade US Army intelligence analyst, described as a loner, a gay in the military, a disgruntled 'computer geek,' sifts through classified information at Forward Operating Base Hammer. He decides to secretly download US State Department email communications from the entire world over a period of eight months for hours a day, onto his blank CDs while pretending to be listening to Lady Gaga. In addition to diplomatic cables, Manning is believed to have provided WikiLeaks with helicopter gun camera video of an errant US attack in Baghdad on unarmed journalists, and with war logs from Iraq and Afghanistan.

Manning then is supposed to have tracked down a notorious former US computer hacker to get his 250,000 pages of classified US State Department cables out in the Internet for the whole world to see. He allegedly told the US hacker that the documents he had contained 'incredible, awful things that belonged in the public domain and not on some server stored in a dark room in Washington, DC.' The hacker turned him in to US authorities so the story goes. Manning is now incommunicado in U.S. military confinement so we cannot ask him, conveniently. The Pentagon routinely hires the best hackers to design their security systems.

Then the plot thickens. The 250,000 pages end up at the desk of Julian Assange, the 39-year-old Australian founder of a supposedly anti-establishment website with the cute name WikiLeaks. Assange decides to selectively choose several of the world's most ultra-establishment news media to exclusively handle the leaking job for him as he seems to be on the run from Interpol, not for leaking classified information, but for allegedly having consensual sex with two Swedish women who later decided it was rape. He selects as exclusive newspapers to decide what is to be leaked the *New York Times* which did such service in promoting faked propaganda against Saddam that led to the Iraqi war, the London *Guardian* and *Der Spiegel*. Assange claims he had no time to sift through so many pages so handed them to the trusted editors of the establishment media for them to decide what should be released. Very 'anti-establishment' that....

Indeed a strange choice of media for a person who claims to be anti-establishment. But then Assange also says he believes the US Government version of 9/11 and calls the Bilderberg Group a normal meeting of people, a very establishment view....

Most important, the 250,000 cables are not 'top secret' as we might have thought. Between two and three million US Government employees are cleared to see this level of 'secret' document, and some 500,000 people around the world have access to the Secret Internet Protocol Network (SIPRnet) where the cables were stored. Siprnet is not recommended for distribution of top-secret information. Only 6% or 15,000 pages of the documents have been classified as even secret, a level below top-secret. Another 40% were the lowest level, 'confidential', while the rest were unclassified. In brief, it was not all that secret....

But for anyone who has studied the craft of intelligence and of disinformation, a clear pattern emerges in the WikiLeaks drama. The focus is put on select US geopolitical targets, appearing as Hillary Clinton put it 'to justify US sanctions against Iran.' They claim North Korea with China's granting of free passage to Korean ships despite US State Department pleas, send dangerous missiles to Iran. Saudi Arabia's ailing King Abdullah reportedly called Iran's President a Hitler.[23]

Another pattern emerges in the WikiLeaks-Bradley Manning drama. The military is trying to deflect focus on how Bradley Manning, or whoever fed him the information, got his hands on the documents, bypassing the most adept military system in the world.

Yes, so, how exactly, *did* a low level employee get access to a classified system? Then, the whole thing gets even wackier. According to the *Guardian* of London,

> On 21 May, a Californian computer hacker called Adrian Lamo was contacted by somebody with the online name Bradass87 who started to swap instant messages with him. He was immediately extraordinarily open: 'hi... how are you?... im an army intelligence analyst, deployed to eastern bagdad ... if you had unprecedented access to classified networks, 14 hours a day, 7 days a week for 8+ months, what would you do?'
>
> For five days, Bradass87 opened his heart to Lamo. He described how his job gave him access to two secret networks: the Secret Internet Protocol Router Network, SIPRNET, which carries US diplomatic and military intelligence classified "secret"; and the Joint Worldwide Intelligence Communications System which uses a different security system to carry similar material classified up to 'top secret'. He said this had allowed him to see 'incredible things, awful things ... that belong in the public domain and not on some server stored in a dark room in Washington DC ... almost criminal political backdealings ... the non-PR version of world events and crises.'
>
> "Bradass87 suggested that 'someone I know intimately' had been downloading and compressing and encrypting all this data and uploading it to someone he identified as Julian Assange. At times, he claimed he himself had leaked the material, suggesting that he had taken in blank CDs, labelled as Lady Gaga's music, slotted them into his high-security laptop and lip-synched to non-existent music to cover his downloading: 'I want people to see the truth,' he said.
>
> He dwelled on the abundance of the disclosure: 'its open diplomacy ... its Climategate with a global scope and breathtaking depth ... its beautiful and horrifying ... It's public data, it belongs in the public domain." At one point, Bradass87 caught himself and said: "i can't believe what im confessing to you." It was too late. Unknown to him, two days into their exchange, on 23 May, Lamo had

contacted the US military. On 25 May he met officers from the Pentagon's criminal investigations department in a Starbucks and gave them a printout of Bradass87's online chat.

On 26 May, at US Forward Operating Base Hammer, 25 miles outside Baghdad, a 22-year-old intelligence analyst named Bradley Manning was arrested, shipped across the border to Kuwait and locked up in a military prison.[24]

Yes, and I am a ham sandwich with a pickle on top. This may sound credible to an uninitiated person, but it's almost a joke in a cyber security world because that's exactly what you do to test the system. It almost seems that it was set up to play itself out this way.

As Cryptome's founder John Young points out when asked about WikiLeaks' spat with Adrian Lamo:

> None of the stuff that Lamo has made available has been verified. Early on, I said chat logs can be forged, you can make this stuff up. So far there's nothing of substance here. It's a story that's being played. I'm not seeing any credible information that this story has any substance at all other than as a story. It's being treated almost as if there's something of substance here because the chat logs have come out. But I've not seen any verification. And chat logs are notoriously (easy to) forge by authorities and other people, as with other digital stuff. So I don't know whether there's anything to this or not. But I'm following it because it's kind of a test of how gullible people can be with a good story. And all frauds work that way.
>
> And I think WikiLeaks is wary too. I think they're not sure that anything's actually happened here or if they're not being sucked into a trap.[25]

Furthermore, there is little proof that the so-called State Department cables actually exist. Has anyone seen them? The answer is no. Has anyone ever asked this question? Silence.

The more one looks at the official story, the more it appears to be a well-orchestrated sting operation. In an interview with CNET, John Young made the following observation: "There was suspicion from day one that this was entrapment run by someone unknown to suck a number of people into a trap. So we actually don't know. But it's certainly a standard counterintelligence technique. And they're usually pretty elaborate and pretty carefully run. They'll even prosecute people as part of the cover story."[26] Bradley Manning may get prosecuted and may even spend some time in jail. Most knowledgeable observers believe, however, that he is a part of the operation and will see relatively little prison time.

Will the status quo try to conceal who was informing and betraying others by pretending to prosecute them. For example,: "High-grade crypto hides any header to avoid disclosing the methodology used. A header may be separately encrypted, coded as blank spaces or punctuation, hidden as innocuous fragments, miniaturized and placed under a digitally-transparent character and other admirably sneaky methods. Other markers are embedded to trace, log and reveal to a recipient evidence of tampering and cracking. Decrypted contents will also contain markers to track distribution and use, and may also contain trojans and/or computer destructors unless disarmed. Whether there is embedded lethality triggerable by misuse is unknown but surely in the works. A dirty trick is to wrap an alluring encrypted package with a transparent trojan in the manner of spam. The endless stream of spam, viruses, searches, bots, clouds, data dumps, advertisements and social media chatter cloak that. What may be wrapped around, hidden and ticking within, infecting, the alluring insurance file is likely to be unpleasant."[27]

Who benefits from that scenario? CyberCom does. They just got huge funding when they were having trouble staying on their feet.

EXCUSE TO POLICE THE INTERNET?

As economist and investigative journalist F. William Engdahl reports, there is a dangerous precedent-setting scenario being played out over the future of Internet.

> What is emerging from all the sound and WikiLeaks fury in Washington is that the entire scandal is serving to advance a long-standing Obama and Bush agenda of policing the until-now free Internet. Already the US Government has shut the WikiLeaks server in the United States though no identifiable US law has been broken.
>
> The process of policing the Web was well underway before the current leaks scandal. In 2009 Democratic Senator Jay Rockefeller and Republican Olympia Snowe introduced the Cybersecurity Act of 2009 (S.773). It would give the President unlimited power to disconnect private-sector computers from the internet. The bill 'would allow the president to 'declare a cyber-security emergency' relating to 'non-governmental' computer networks and do what's necessary to respond to the threat.' We can expect that this controversial piece of legislation will get top priority now when a new Republican House and the Senate convene in January.
>
> The US Department of Homeland Security, an agency created in the political hysteria following 9/11 2001 that has been compared to the Gestapo, has already begun policing the Internet. They are quietly seizing and shutting down internet websites (web domains) without due process or a proper trial. DHS simply seizes web domains that it wants to and posts an ominous "Department of Justice" logo on the web site. See an example at http:// torrent-finder.com. Over 75 websites were seized and shut in a recent week. Right now, their focus is websites that they claim 'violate copyrights,' yet the torrent-finder. com website that was seized by DHS contained no copyrighted content whatsoever. It was merely a search engine website that linked to destinations where people could access copyrighted content. Step by careful step freedom of speech can be taken away. Then what?[28]

THE SHADOW GOVERNMENT

Ed Encho reports in OpEdNews.com:

Suppose that the United States Government, or more likely an unaccountable privatized intelligence colossus empowered by the reaction to the 9/11 attacks and fueled by the rampant cronyism of a system long ago gone rotten had a surveillance tool capable of peering into the most private aspects of American lives on a whim. Now suppose that the new growth industry of a previously unthinkable futuristic police state was already in place, is fully operational and has in fact been online and has been actively utilized for illegal domestic spying purposes for years, and that it was being used well before those two airplanes slammed into the World Trade Center. The 'terrorist' attacks were then and have been used as the justification for every unconstitutional reigning in of civil liberties ever since that heinous September morning seven years ago when the reset button was hit on two and a quarter centuries of American history and we all stepped forth into the brave new world of perpetual war, fear, suspicion and vengeance into a parallel reality in a place that would come to be ominously known as *The Homeland*. What if this surveillance industrial complex was in possession of a database that was so large and so powerful that not only could it instantly process and retrieve the most minute or intimate aspects of a citizen's lives but was also able to utilize extremely sophisticated artificial intelligence capabilities to actually predict likely patterns of future behavior."

Such a huge database would be able to use cutting edge technology funded with taxpayer dollars and awarded to unaccountable private corporations largely through 'business as usual' no bid contracts to create the most invasive tool of oppression this country has ever seen. This database would rely on software that was capable of performing social network analysis based on block modeling technology to monitor all forms of electronic communications, all internet searches, all debit and credit card transactions, all travel arrangements, all library records, all bank activity and all telephone records. It would then be able to use the data to not only find links between persons who already know and interact with each other but to categorize each individual into a particular group that possess similar behavioral and purchasing habits.

These groups could then be further divided into subgroups and further analyzed in order to determine under some loosely defined and largely unknown guidelines whether they could potentially represent a threat. While all of this may sound like some sort of futuristic dystopian nightmare straight out of Philip K. Dick's *Minority Report* and 'Pre-crime' it is very real and it goes by the name of Main Core. For example, if you are selling a bicycle and run an advertisement in your local newspaper and you happen to receive a call from a Muhammad who is interested in your bicycle and Muhammad happens to have certain friends who have relationships with an organization that is determined by some unknown criteria to be a potential terrorist organization then the call that you received from Muhammad would then in all likelihood place you in the database and subject to an increased level of scrutiny at best and at worst in jeopardy of being picked up and held indefinitely without any sort of judicial review.

This technology is being used today absent any form of legitimate oversight, with a Constitution that has been eviscerated by the Bush-Cheney-Rove Axis of Evil, a vast gulag network of top secret prisons and 'detention facilities' and the decidedly anti-American new phenomenon of state sanctioned torture. Throw in an overworked, systematically dumbed-down populace that has been propagandized by the corrupt institution that is the corporate media machine with it's clever use of fear and loathing and scientific development of advanced mind control techniques who despite the infinite wisdom of our forefathers would gladly sacrifice their liberty for the any sort of temporary safety (no matter that it is fleeting) and there exists today in 'The Homeland' a perfect petri dish for an authoritarian fascist society.

It is though a very sophisticated form of fascism unlike more outwardly obvious regimes that we have known in the past. Author Bertram Gross published a book back in 1980 that was entitled *Friendly Fascism*, Jim Garrison once said that "fascism would come to America in the name of national security," and author Kevin Phillips in his 1983 book *Post-Conservative America* warned of the potential of an 'apple pie authoritarianism' and a coming society in which: 'the Star Spangled Banner would wave with greater frequency and over many more parades; increased surveillance would crack down on urban outbreaks and extreme political dissidents'. This very accurately describes post 9/11 America where any semblance of reason has been abandoned for cheap flag-waving pimped off as patriotism, criticism of authority has made into potential treason by the highly paid shills for neoconservative doctrine, sloganeering and demagoguery have replaced discourse, critical thinking is becoming extinct and just as George Orwell so accurately predicted Big Brother is now watching over us, protecting us and ensuring that we understand that war is peace, freedom is slavery and ignorance is strength.[29]

Is there any proof that WikiLeaks is being used as an excuse to police the Internet?

According to a number of experts, WikiLeaks may well be "a theatre operation. Partly lulling, partly testing systems. Testing public reaction, are we going to get traction out of cyber threats or not. Will this work or not, because as you know they (WikiLeaks) haven't caused any harm that is why they haven't been charged... and then there will be some lives lost or something will happen... and at some point when this cyber war becomes a real war, we will see because the laws will be ready."[30]

CYBER SECURITY COMMAND (CYBERCOM)

In every theatre operation, you have one or two main players and a bunch of secondary actors who enter and exit the stage, depending on the development of the play itself. And that's where CyberCom comes in.

In reality, Cyber Command, which is meant to deal with new threats, is a public relations stunt by the Defense Department. The program is still run by the NSA. The head of CyberCom, is also the head of National Security Agency. According to the United States government, cyber threats will eventually replace terrorist threats. We are hearing more and more how terrorists are planning Internet attacks on us, so this is a kind of melding of the two threats into one. There is an easily visible pattern here.

The accusations of Congressional members that WikiLeaks is a threat is exactly part of that pattern, a repeat of the Red Menace and all kinds of other fabricated menaces. Now, they have a fabulous opportunity to say that the enemy is already inside the US and on the Internet.

"An increasing clamor to restrict and control the internet on behalf of the government, the Pentagon, the intelligence community and their private corporate arms, could result in a staged cyber attack which will be used as justification"[31] for government's policing the internet or in the worst case scenario, shutting it down, warn numerous security experts, government sources, high ranking members of the intelligence community and privacy advocates in the United States.

Since 9/11, Homeland Security (DHS) and the Pentagon have worked together to monitor and subvert the real threat to the government — political activists and organizations within the United States. "In addition to snooping anti-war organizations, the DHS has worked overtime (with a complaisant corporate media) to portray the patriot movement as violent and a threat to national security."[32]

It wouldn't be long before DHS and the Pentagon came up with a perfect antidote for "the ruling elite's overall and over-reaching control grid"[33] – Cyber Command. "In order to fight against the growing number of people now awake to their agenda, our rulers must take out the independent media on the internet,"[34] the last remaining source of unrestricted free speech. As Kurt Nimmo points out on *infowars. com*: "The Pentagon's Cyber Command was not established to fight Somalian or al-Qaeda hackers in remote backwater caves — or China and Russia for that matter. It was established to fight the real enemy — the American people."[35]

In the age of Global Political Awakening, we, the people, have become the enemy. Zbigniew Brzezinski, a member of the Bilderberg Group, Council on Foreign Relations, and a co-founder of the Trilateral Commission with banker David Rockefeller in 1973, "has written extensively on the issue of the 'Global Political Awakening,' and has been giving speeches at various elite think tanks around the world, 'informing' the elites of this changing global dynamic. Brzezinski is one of the principle representatives of the global elite and one of the most influential establishment intellectuals in the world. His analysis of the 'global political awakening' is useful because of his representation of it as the primary global threat to elite interests everywhere. Thus, people should view the concept of the 'global political awakening' as the greatest potential hope for humanity and that it should be advanced and aided, as opposed to Brzezinski's perspective that it should be controlled and suppressed. However, it would be best for Brzezinski to explain the concept in his own words to allow people to understand how it constitutes a 'threat' to elite interests:

> For the first time in human history almost all of humanity is politically activated, politically conscious and politically interactive. There are only a few pockets of humanity left in the remotest corners of the world that are not politically alert and engaged with the political turmoil and stirrings that are so widespread today around the world. The resulting global political activism is generating a surge in the quest for personal dignity, cultural

165

respect and economic opportunity in a world painfully scarred by memories of centuries-long alien colonial or imperial domination... The worldwide yearning for human dignity is the central challenge inherent in the phenomenon of global political awakening.

'...America needs to face squarely a centrally important new global reality: that the world's population is experiencing a political awakening unprecedented in scope and intensity, with the result that the politics of populism are transforming the politics of power. The need to respond to that massive phenomenon poses to the uniquely sovereign America an historic dilemma: What should be the central definition of America's global role? ... The central challenge of our time is posed not by global terrorism, but rather by the intensifying turbulence caused by the phenomenon of global political awakening. That awakening is socially massive and politically radicalizing.

'... It is no overstatement to assert that now in the 21st century the population of much of the developing world is politically stirring and in many places seething with unrest. It is a population acutely conscious of social injustice to an unprecedented degree, and often resentful of its perceived lack of political dignity. The nearly universal access to radio, television and increasingly the Internet is creating a community of shared perceptions and envy that can be galvanized and channeled by demagogic political or religious passions. These energies transcend sovereign borders and pose a challenge both to existing states as well as to the existing global hierarchy, on top of which America still perches.

'... The youth of the Third World are particularly restless and resentful. The demographic revolution they embody is thus a political time-bomb, as well. With the exception of Europe, Japan and America, the rapidly expanding demographic bulge in the 25-year-old-and-under age bracket is creating a huge mass of impatient young people. Their minds have been stirred by sounds and images that emanate from afar and which intensify their disaffection with what is at hand. Their potential

166

revolutionary spearhead is likely to emerge from among the scores of millions of students concentrated in the often intellectually dubious "tertiary level" educational institutions of developing countries. Depending on the definition of the tertiary educational level, there are currently worldwide between 80 and 130 million "college" students. Typically originating from the socially insecure lower middle class and inflamed by a sense of social outrage, these millions of students are revolutionaries-in-waiting, already semi-mobilized in large congregations, connected by the Internet and pre-positioned for a replay on a larger scale of what transpired years earlier in Mexico City or in Tiananmen Square. Their physical energy and emotional frustration is just waiting to be triggered by a cause, or a faith, or a hatred.[36]

The 'growing cyber threat' hyped by the government and the corporate media is merely cover for the real agenda. The agenda is that "WikiLeaks is a big and dangerous US intelligence Con Job that will likely be used to police the Internet."[37]

For example, in July 2010, the "U.S. Strategic Command [held] "a cyberspace symposium in Omaha, Nebraska."[38] According to a press release, "This event provides an exciting venue for information exchange among leaders in Cyberspace. Fostering innovation and collaboration between the private sector and government to delve into tough cyber issues will be paramount for this symposium. The symposium [was] sponsored by Lockheed Martin, HP, Booz Allen Hamilton, CACI, Cisco, CSC, General Dynamics, QinetiQ, Raytheon and the spooky MITRE Corporation."[39]

Half of these corporations are full-time members of the Bilderberg Group. Most of them form part of the Council on Foreign Relations.

> The Pentagon considers cyberspace a 'warfighting domain' equal to land, sea, air and space. In 2003, the Pentagon classified the Internet as an enemy 'weapons system' requiring a robust offensive suite of capabilities to include full-range electronic and computer network attack.

In short, the mission of the Cyber Command will be primarily offensive, not defensive. Bush ... Def. Sec. Robert Gates ordered the creation of the Cyber Command in June of 2009 specifically in response to the "already significant and growing digital threat" from "foreign actors, terrorists, criminal groups and individual hackers, according to the *Air Force Times*."[40]

The hype for a terrorist cyber attack is becoming deafening. Over recent months we have seen dire reports issued by the Defense Science Board and the Center for Strategic and International Studies over a possible 'electronic Pearl Harbor' and 'cyber-Katrina' events, with reports claiming that a "Cyber attack 'could fell US within 15 minutes.'"[41]

Given the now infamous Tony Blair remarks about Saddam Hussein's weapons of mass destruction and a 45-minute launch, few people take the reports seriously.

What is undeniable, is "that much of the data on the supposed cyber threat are gathered by ultra-secretive government agencies — which need to justify their own existence — and cyber-security companies — which derive commercial benefits from popular anxiety."[42] Thus, the meeting in Nebraska in July 2010, attended by the leading corporations in the sector. "Large corporations such as Google, AT&T, Facebook and Yahoo to name but a few are intimately involved in the overarching program. Those corporations have specific government arms that are supplying the software, hardware and tech support to US intelligence agencies in the process of creating a vast closed source database for global spy networks to share information."[43]

When the Cybersecurity Act was introduced by Senator John Rockefeller in April of 2009, he openly asked whether it would have been better if we'd never invented the Internet? The "bill to establish the Office of the National Cybersecurity Advisor—an arm of the executive branch that would have vast power to monitor and control Internet traffic to protect against threats to critical cyber infrastructure"[44] encountered virtually no opposition from the mainstream press, not even from such left-wing libertarian organizations as Truth in the Media, whose reason to be is exactly that – protecting the freedom of speech of the Fourth Estate.

> Rockefeller's legislation gives the president the ability to declare a cybersecurity emergency, and hand absolute power to the federal government to shut down networks, and block incoming Internet traffic in the interest of national security....[45]

A *Wall Street Journal* blog reports that the bill would allow the federal government, through the Department of Homeland Security and the NSA to gather information from "all Internet communications, including the contents of emails"[46] without a warrant. As Investigative journalist Steve Watson reports: "banking, business and medical records would be wide open to inspection, as well as personal instant message and e-mail communications – all in the name of heading off cyber attacks on the nation." Say hello to the real Big Brother.

Writes Kurt Nimmo in *infowars.com*: "NSA Director Lt. Gen. Keith Alexander told the Senate Armed Services Committee in April [2010] that he would work ... 'we comport, comply with the laws,' and protect the privacy rights of Americans."[47] "Alexander said the Pentagon's Cyber Command would enjoy 'significant synergy' with the NSA.[48] Interesting comments from a newly appointed head of Cyber Command, a subordinate unified command under United States Strategic Command "designed to conduct virtual combat across the world's computer networks,.[49]

The Electronic Frontier Foundation reports: The U.S. government with assistance from major telecommunications carriers including AT&T has engaged in a massive program of illegal dragnet surveillance of domestic communications and communications records of millions of ordinary Americans since at least 2001.[50]

Welcome to the New World Order. "The Pentagon considers cyberspace a warfighting domain equal to land, sea, air and space. In 2003, the Pentagon classified the Internet as an enemy 'weapons system' requiring a 'robust offensive suite of capabilities to include full-range electronic and computer network attack.' It has spent Billions of dollars building a super secret 'National Cyber Range' in order to prepare for 'Dominant Cyber Offensive Engagement,' which translates as control over 'any and all' computers. The program has been dubbed 'The Electronic Manhattan Project.'"[51]

It is unnerving that the so-called "enemy is never ... named, it is merely whoever uses the net, because the enemy *is* the net. The enemy is the freedom the net provides to billions around the globe and the threat to militaristic dominance of information and the ultimate power that affords.

> These initiatives represent a continuation of the so-called 'Comprehensive National Cybersecurity Initiative', created via a secret presidential order in 2008 under the Bush administration. Former National Intelligence Director Mike McConnell announced that the NSA's warrantless wiretaps would 'be a walk in the park compared to this.'[52]

As part of this Initiative, the Air Force in the summer of 2010 "assigned approximately 30,000 'digital troops' to 'the front lines of cyber warfare,' a number that represents a third of the troops in Afghanistan ... reported the *Air Force Times* on May 19."[53]

WHAT ABOUT THE POISON PILL?

But there is another aspect to the NSA-Cyber Command-Bradley Manning-WikiLeaks we need to examine.

An August 7, 2010 AP article (which is no longer available for download) asked in its title:

Is WikiLeaks Bluffing NSA to Spill Its AES Backdoor Secrets

At the center of the drama was the posting of a massive 1.4 gigabyte mystery file named '"Insurance" [the so-called 'poison pill'] on the WikiLeaks website. The password would be released if Assange were arrested, killed, or WikiLeaks was shut down. The 'Insurance' file is encrypted, nearly impossible to open until WikiLeaks provides the passwords. The National Security Agency (NSA) has known about the file for months: Assange uploaded the file in July to WikiLeaks' Afghan War Diaries page, as if challenging hackers to break in. But experts suggest that if anyone can crack it — it would be the National Security Agency. It depends on how much time and effort they want to put into it, said James Bamford, who has written two books on the NSA.

The NSA has the largest collection of supercomputers in the world. And officials have known for some time that WikiLeaks has classified files in its possession. The agency, he speculated, has probably been looking for a vulnerability or gap in the code, or a backdoor into the commercial encryption program protecting the file.

At the more extreme end, the NSA, the Pentagon and other U.S. government agencies — including the newly created Cyber Command — have probably reviewed options for using a cyber attack against the website, which could disrupt networks, files, electricity, and so on. "This is the kind of thing that they are geared for," said Bamford, "since this is the type of thing a terrorist organization might have — a website that has damaging information on it. They would want to break into it, see what's there and then try to destroy it."

The vast nature of the Internet, however, makes it essentially impossible to stop something, or take it down, once it has gone out over multiple servers. In the end, U.S. officials will have to weigh whether a more aggressive response is worth the public outrage it would likely bring. Most experts predict that, despite the uproar, the government will probably do little other than bluster, and the documents will come out anyway.

171

Once you start messing with the Internet, taking things down, and going to the maximum extent to hide everything from coming out, it doesn't necessarily serve your purpose," said Bamford. 'It makes the story bigger than it would have been had the documents been released in the first place. If, in the end, the goal is to decrease the damage, you have to wonder whether pouring fuel on the fire is a reasonable solution,' he said.[54]

Is WikiLeaks being played or does it moonlight for another intelligence agency wanting to track NSA's capabilities? Is this science fiction or reality?

Cryptome's founder John Young points out:

Information security (with communications security) protects the most valuable secrets on earth -- defence operational plans, weapons of mass destruction technology, intelligence, and government perfidy, among others. Encryption plays a vital role along with subterfuge about capabilities for offence and defensive information warfare. Deception and ploys abound. Attacks and counterattacks test for vulnerability, using means more powerful than an expected enemy. Insiders and outsiders are employed to test continuously, the unorthodox and orthodox. The witting and unwitting are drawn into tests by falling for lures set up for that purpose. A target may recognise a lure and pretend to fall for it to assay a defender's capabilities, and that may lead to a counter-subterfuge, and so on. Cryptography and cryptanalysis battle without end. Bribing the other side is a favorite tactic; disparaging prowess to incite a spasm of vainglorious disclosure another.[55]

Delving into tech speak, Young explained that,

A common infosec subterfuge is to use every notable occasion to claim a system is invulnerable in order to promote continued use of the system. NSA has run a number of these disinformation campaigns about 'unbreakable' encryption, secret (German, Japanese, Soviet, et al) and public – the most famous public system involved Crypto

AG, within whose cryptosystem NSA installed a backdoor to gain access to communications of world-wide users who believed the system was invulnerable.

Doubts about the invulnerability of AES have persisted since NSA selected an algorithm from an AES competition that was considered by cryptographers not to be the strongest. And that it is likely for strongest protection NSA uses a top secret cryptosystem while promoting AES for public and official use. It is argued that NSA, like all official comsec agencies, would never endorse a system it could not secretly access. And these agencies never reveal that capability – NSA's backdoor access to Crypto AG was revealed by an employee of the company.

Bet that NSA has cracked the insurance file and is keeping quiet. NSA may have replaced the file with its own when it first appeared – WikiLeaks long on instant crypto radar – the hash forged, covertly marked for tracking. Bluff becomes bait for entrapment, SOP.

Could WikiLeaks have intended to entrap NSA and allies with a crackable file, covertly marked for tracking? Some of WikiLeaks infosec-comsec advisors do top-classified work for the US and other governments. A very handsome sum would be quietly paid for that service. Cyberwarfare secrets are yet to be spilled, never to be revealed in courts. Fierce dirty combat could do that, unless the combatants reach a secret deal to share the benefits of dual use technology while pretending to be at odds, SOP.[56]

"The security watchword is: don't ever expect infallible security that is always snail oil. The intelligence watchword is never trust an intelligence source, they are all unreliable. The classification watchword is never trust the highest classification, that is bullshovel to dupe those who believe only they have access."[57]

The "sysadmin" watchword is ... lay low, log everything, copy, replace with a fake, tell no one; especially another sysadmin who will rat you.

THE FUTURE OF WHISTLEBLOWING

"Psychopathy likely is one of those many glitches in the gene pool, an evolutionary trial-and-error that served a useful purpose before modern urban society, psychopathic warriors being valued for their ability at defending early human settlements and terrifying potential enemies. Probably most of our legends of monsters such as vampires or ghouls derive from human experience with all-too-real psychopathic personalities."[58]

"In psychology and psychoanalysis, reality testing is the technique of objective evaluation of an emotion or thought against real life, as a faculty present in normal individuals but defective in some psychotics."[59] In politics, 'real life' is compressed into a small number of people who dedicate their time to cunning selfishness.

"Politics is not an end, but a means." Calvin Coolidge once noted, "It is not a product, but a process. It is the art of government. Like other values it has its counterfeits. So much emphasis has been placed upon the false that the significance of the true has been obscured and politics has come to convey the meaning of crafty and cunning selfishness, instead of candid and sincere service."[60]

As I said in my 2005 Bilderberg report, *Breaking the Silence*, "If democracy is the rule of the 'free' people, secret government agendas and influence-peddling sinister cliques are incompatible with democracy. The whole idea of clandestine spheres lest we wish to repeat the fatal errors of the not-so-distant past."[61]

One of the ways in which government abuse of power is checked, is through whistleblowers. Until the appearance of WikiLeaks, a whistleblower was a person who brought to light alleged government, public or private misconduct. "In its best form, it is performed by individuals in all their great variety and ingenuity of imagination, communication, argumentation and conviction without intervention by interest-biased mediators"[62] ... and should be encouraged as a civic responsibility.

It has been a part of the American justice system since "the 1863 United States False Claims Act, which tried to combat fraud by suppliers of the United States government during the Civil War."[63]

"Whistleblowing, which has many open and surreptitious forms other than leaks, should be seen as a necessary opposition to increasing secrecy and confidentiality in government, commerce and biased institutions;"[64] it should be varied and widespread around the world and independent of government. "For this, the Internet is a grand, wild experiment, which will always be threatened by unaccountable managers, censorship, contamination, exploitation, take-over, even takedown, by those who want to control and profit from information and communications by secrecy and confidentiality."[65] In this sense, WikiLeaks, if it is used properly, poses a mortal danger to the Empire.

There is little doubt that WikiLeaks is changing the world. However these changes "must be conceptualized within our understanding of the geopolitical reality we find ourselves in today.... As has been the case both historically and presently, imperial objectives are hidden with political rhetoric."[66] WikiLeaks seems to represent the reality of the diplomatic social group and thus they are a vivid exploration in the study of imperialism.

The Soviet Union fell. The Berlin Wall fell. China became increasingly capitalist. Vietnam has become America's partner for peace. The enemies that the Republicans had warned about since 1945 were now disappearing. The Red Menace and the Yellow Peril were things of the past. We even witnessed the shocking scene of Brent Scowcroft, former United States National Security Adviser, in Beijing a month after the Tiananmen Square episode in 1989, toasting the Chinese leaders at the request of self-proclaimed China expert and former Ambassador to China (briefly) President George H.W. Bush. Although America laid sanctions against China for the Tiananmen "massacre," Bush ensured that his older brother – Prescott, Jr. – was still able to broker a deal between the Chinese government and Hughes Aircraft for the sale of communications satellites, when other American companies were barred from so doing. It was a New World Order, indeed. The Republicans had made the world safe for... well, Republicans.

And it is precisely because of this unaccountability and corruption that WikiLeaks' current popularity and momentum must be placed within a wider context and understanding. As Andrew Gavin Marshall writes in his well-researched essay on the WikiLeaks phenomenon, "The reports from WikiLeaks are 'revelation' only to those who largely adhere to the 'illusions' of the world: that we live in 'democracies' promoting 'freedom' around the world and at home."[67]

Without a doubt, explains John Young in a *Culture Show* interview with the BBC, WikiLeaks and what it represents,

> ...is a very valuable step in the right direction but more outlets are needed that do not require secrecy and confidentiality of their operation – these practices mirror those of authorities. There are risks to being open and identifiable, but operating in secrecy is not the only answer.... Confidential leaks have become a tool for disseminating contaminated information, whether by government, commerce, institutions or individuals. Due to the growth in the lucrative and ego-boosting leakage industry, leaks have become suspect as a reliable source of information.
>
> "Alone [leaks] are treacherous.... 'Anonymous sources,' 'revealed by those not authorised to speak about the matter,' 'unnamed officials,' and leakage are now brands used to promote products as if credible and worthy when their principal purpose is to vaunt the reputation of the source and the outlet. There are quite effective if subtler and intellectually demanding ways than leaks to reliably provide to the public prohibited information.... Attention should be paid to the multitude of transparent sources of information to diminish the misleading allure of confidential leaks. Leaks need capacious context from open sources to understand and judge their significance.[68]

Secret and confidential information is never reliable because it leads to closed and self-deluded intelligence (intellectual and spy product). In that sense, leaks, which are bred by secrecy and confidentiality, are suspect, due to their restricted provenance. Leaks only become believable by placing them in a reliable open source context, challenge and debate, which it should be recalled, was the original intention of WikiLeaks, hence its original open wiki aspect now abandoned in favour of assertion (WikiLeaks has commented on its lack of public wikiness).[69]

In this sense, "WikiLeaks is a globally transformative event. Not simply in terms of awakening people to 'new' information, but also in terms of the effect it is having upon global power structures, itself. With ambassadors resigning, diplomats being exposed as liars and tools, political rifts developing between Western imperial allies, and many careers and reputations of elites around the world at great risk, WikiLeaks is creating the potential for an enormous deterioration in the effectiveness of imperialism and domination. That, in itself, is an admirable and worthy goal. That this is already a reality is representative of how truly transformative WikiLeaks is and could have been. People, globally, are starting to see their leaders through a lens not filtered by 'public relations.'"[70]

We would be wise to understand that threats to democracy come from the secret keepers. Without a doubt, because of WikiLeaks, "systems and structures of power around the world are in the process of being exposed to a much wider audience than ever before."[71] Without a doubt that is the reason "we are under a heavy propaganda offensive on the part of the global corporate and mainstream media to spin and manipulate these leaks to their own interests.... The mainstream media understood that from the very beginning.... WikiLeaks presents in itself a further opportunity for the larger exposure of mainstream media as organized propaganda. By 'surprising' so many people with the 'revelations,' the media has in effect exposed itself as deeply inadequate in their analysis of the world and the major issues within it."[72]

*****

While Romanticism may be dead, a curiosity fit only for English Literature courses and tenured professors in tweedy jackets and elbow patches, there is a new kind of Romantic element at play in the West because of WikiLeaks. There is a growing realization that we cannot depict what really happened without an element of the novelistic. We can't tell the story without...telling a story. The initial story of WikiLeaks was love at first sight. As Assange himself had said, "we start to see community involvement, which digs deeper and provides more perspective. So the social networks tend to be, for us, an amplifier of what we are doing."[73]

Writer Andrew Gavin Marshall poignantly points out, "As researchers, media, and critics, we realized that our perspectives and beliefs were being opened to change and evolution. Simply because something like this has never happened before does not mean that it isn't happening now. We live in the era of the 'Technological Revolution,' and the Internet has changed economics, politics and society itself, on a global scale. This is where the true hope in furthering and better informing the 'global political awakening' will need to take speed and establish itself. True change in our world is not going to come from already-established or newly created institutions of power, which is where all issues are currently being addressed, especially those of global significance. True change, instead, can only come not from global power structures, but from the global 'community' of people, interacting with one another via the power unleashed by the 'Technological Revolution.' In the age of global social transformation, change must be globally understood and community organized. The question is will we do anything about it?"[74]

What has obsessed me in these pages is not the paranoia of the clerk, but of the congressman. Of the President, and the Pentagon. Of five-star generals and CIA directors and FBI profilers. This is not the paranoia of the loser, of the victim – pathetic, understandable – but of the winner, the victor: The paranoia of the people in charge. People who should know better, and probably do. It is what they fear most that I fear most: what they do not want us to know. The paranoia of experts. After all, if you are not paranoid, you don't know all the facts.

It is the paranoia of men who shred documents in the executive offices at CIA headquarters, like schoolboys hiding a dirty magazine.

There is blood, and there are documents. This is history. You can't have one without the other. Blood. Documents. Guilt. Innocence. Knowledge. Ignorance. Frustration. Fear. But you can't know history unless you know fear. You can't know history unless you feel the pulse of life under your fingers; unless you can stare the guns in the face. Unless you can stand in the prisons, and the death camps, and feel the gaze of informers and spies and soldiers on your back in foreign countries…and on your own doorstep, your own driveway. History is not to be absent but to become missing; to be someone and then go away, leaving only traces. The rest then, is only bookkeeping.

The world has always been like this, of course. It has always been run by: superstitious, religious, fearful, paranoid, ugly, hateful, murderous people. That is nothing new. But at a specific point in the century we took this a step further. With WikiLeaks, we opened Pandora's box, and the black box of human consciousness. We flipped open the lid, and rummaged around inside. And we unearthed monsters.

With WikiLeaks, one comes to the conclusion that there is nowhere to go, no one to trust. But can the source itself, be trusted and taken at their word? To answer that question one would have to read stacks of books, mountains of references to be cross-checked and verified in virtually every discipline known: political science, history, archaeology, paleo-astronomy, occultism, psychology, philosophy, physics, medicine, chemistry, anthropology, Watergate, Pentagon Papers, Wall Street, assassinations, intelligence programs, Hollywood, military history. Did we miss anything? Hundreds of thousands of books, piles upon piles of documents. Is it any wonder, after all that – the shots that changed the world, that martyred a President, that ended a reign of hope, that brought us Vietnam, Iran-Contra, drugs, 9/11, Afghanistan, Iraq, Iran, Color revolutions, financial disintegration and a new Cold War – were said to have come from a place where books were stored?

CNN brought us "made for TV wars." Reality became entertainment, became reality when American soldiers were captured, killed or paraded in front of home audiences. What does it all mean? We have to put events in context for them to have any meaning, the same way a homicide detective examines the clues at the scene of the crime; and it is precisely this insistence on meaning that has plagued realism from the start, and has led to the confrontation between this world and the parallel universe of smoke and mirrors. And in the midst of that confrontation, wandering the labyrinth of cults between what is mainstream and what is fringe conspiracies and their colorful, underworld characters, an abyss of politics by other means, be it mind control, LSD, the occult, secret societies, powerful private organizations, foundations, religion, intelligence agencies, expendable whistleblowers like Bradley Manning and a new 'brotherhood buried alive' of 'no future' generations, we find ex-hacker Julian Assange and his parallel WikiLeaks world.

We could sum up with a quotation from the late, lamented Walt Kelley's Pogo comic strip: "We have met the enemy and he is us." Once we realize this, we can begin to make America the place of greatness and beauty and transcendence that it was intended to be, intended to be by our founding fathers who were, after all, Freemasons and Rosicrucians and Templars and freethinkers and mystics, who believed in spiritual regeneration and psychological integration."[75]

As I write these closing remarks, the world is facing a financial meltdown unprecedented in the annals of history. The elite power circles of the United States are literally an empire standing on feet of clay and sinking. The American economy, which had been but sixty years earlier the envy of the world, by the end of the first decade of the new century, was a debt-bloated, de-industrialized and largely bankrupt shadow of its former self, for as much as the corporate media tried to soften the blow and divert our attention to other, less pernicious matters. The American financial system is choking on trillions of dollars in worthless securitized credits they had underwritten in the last great binge of the real estate bubble of 2002-2007.

The only remaining option for the power elites of Washington to hold on to their global power was to project their military force – Full Spectrum Dominance. The pressures of an increasingly desperate US foreign policy were forcing an unlikely "coalition of the unwilling" across the entire world. From Uzbekistan to Kyrgyzstan, from Tajikistan to China, from the oil rich Venezuela, Iran and Kazakhstan, China and Russia began to view this coalition as a counterweight to increasingly arbitrary American power politics. The missing link was the military security that could make it less vulnerable to the bully tactics from NATO and Washington. Only one power on earth has the nuclear and military base and know-how to provide that – Russia.

> As of January 2006, Russia possessed 927 nuclear delivery vehicles and 4,279 nuclear warheads against 1,255 and 5,966 respectively for the United States. No two other powers on the face of the earth even came close to these massive overkill capacities. This was the ultimate reason all US foreign policy, military and economic, since the end of the Cold War had covertly had as endgame the complete deconstruction of Russia as a functioning state.

181

Bush's America, a hollowed-out debt-ridden economy engaged on using its last card, its vast military power to prop up the dollar and its role as the sole Superpower. It was the most precarious confluence of forces and events the world had perhaps ever confronted. Until suddenly, WikiLeaks intervened and history began re-writing itself fibre by fibre and one human story at a time, nudging the truth, ever so slowly and painfully, into the light of day.[76]

At first, WikiLeaks stunned the world by showing us the degree to which it was all being acted out behind military jargon, reckless abandon and suppressed strategic debate in the United States and most of the Western Europe. It simply boggles the mind. Until WikiLeaks came onto the scene, scarcely anyone had the slightest idea just how dangerous the madness driving Washington policy had become. Most of the secrets are still hidden in inaccessible vaults, behind double Top Secret classification.

The depth and degree of the homicidal intent of Full Spectrum Dominance reaches much further into our nightmare. The existence of these groups gives us the opportunity to witness what they could do when expanded outside American territory, far from the reach of Congress and a disinterested electorate. We can see what these programs were intended to do, as they developed, untrammeled, in the African bush and Latin American killing fields. We can peer behind the apologetic shrugs and embarrassed smiles of CIA director Richard Helms before Congressional investigators, and go right to where the fruits of their labours were being harvested. How else to really understand what MK-ULTRA and all those acronyms were all about unless we see them in action? How else to visualize the true nature of "fifty years of ideological conflict" mentioned by Scaife unless we watch some of the combatants, the same people who would conduct pious crusades against Clinton, JFK, Martin Luther King Jr., against the people and the places nobody knew existed on the map, for real or imagined wrongs?

"That first Sunday in June 1968," writes Peter Levenda in his trilogy *Sinister Forces*,

> ... at the funeral for Robert Kennedy – the last best hope for a renewed America for a long time to come – his brother, Senator Edward Kennedy, read the eulogy. It contained Bobby's favorite quotation, one that he would use to revive his flagging spirits or to raise the energy of his followers.
>
> It is a beautiful sentiment, but how many listeners in St. Patrick's Cathedral in Manhattan that solemn spring day realized the original context? As Bobby's body lay in the centre aisle of that Gothic pile, surrounded by those who loved and admired him, his "robopathic" assassin in jail in Los Angeles staring stupidly around him in confusion, the men who authorised the murder toasting themselves in comfort in the boardrooms and living rooms and conference rooms and bedrooms of America, some of them even there, in the church watching the funeral service with cynical satisfaction, knowing that the assassination had taken place and that America was ripe for the plunder, the words of their sinister god were being quoted as epitaph:
>
> You see things; and you say, "Why?" But I dream things that never were; and I say "Why not?"
>
> The quote comes from George Bernard Shaw's *Back to Methuselah*, and they are the words of the Devil.[77]

Am I being paranoid? Is it all much simpler than I am making things out to be? Or is it a question of questioning a questioner? Is it even necessary? Convenient? Advisable? Where did WikiLeaks go astray? Or did it? Again and again, I keep coming back to the same question. Am I being paranoid? Is it justifiable? "Skepticism, not paranoia, about the Internet and digital communication in general is self-protective because their managers and operators are inaccessible to public scrutiny under claims of secrecy and confidentiality, and are therefore publicly unaccountable."[78] Nothing new in this, skepticism about secret authority is an ancient counter to abuse of privilege and trust.

Since bursting onto the scene five years ago, Assange and WikiLeaks have become icons, an archetype of confluent forces. It is also a very real story of espionage, mind control and politics. By encoding WikiLeaks in a vast media machine, the mainstream press has usurped most of their power. This is not to say that this power is evil in and of itself; that would be naive. The power of the media (and WikiLeaks has become just another media outlet) should be respected for what it is, a kind of institutionalized or industrialized mind control. No truth, only the decadence of power. The world's elite and their Puppet Masters do not want us to think independently, they want our consciousness massaged by the old, familiar rituals, slogans and clichés. Their tools are the tools of psychological warfare: mind control and behavioral control.

The motto of the CIA, world's foremost expert in mind control and brainwashing is: "You shall know the Truth, and the Truth will set you free." No truth in an empty slogan, however. Only the decadence of power.

Over the time span of working on this book, I came to realize that WikiLeaks had almost become the new religion of America, and, to a certain extent, of the rest of the world as well. It's Hollywood, starring Julian Assange, where he could be seen and heard and touched by the masses; not only in Hollywood, of course, but also in New York, Europe, Moscow, Brazil, Venezuela, China, Pakistan, Afghanistan, Japan, Iran and so on. Americans emulate stars more than they do the saints of their religions: they dress like them, drive the same cars, have the same attitudes, talk like them, cut their hair in the same manner as their favorite stars, and even adopt the same cultural mores.

Pop Culture, in fact, has given status to the "celebrity" which few serious men attain. And what is a "celebrity" if not the ultimate human pseudo-event, fabricated on purpose to satisfy our exaggerated expectations of human greatness. This is the ultimate success story of the twenty-first century and its pursuit of illusion. "A new mold has been made … so that marketable human models—modern heroes—could be mass-produced, to satisfy the market, and without any hitches. The qualities which now commonly make a man or woman into a 'nationally advertised' brand are in fact a new category of human emptiness."[79]

The world we have been peering into is somehow beyond good and evil. It is a world of sentimentality, of makeovers, of people who are willing to shed a tear just before a commercial break, or write a "tell-all-book" with yet another bombshell of publicity and then return with uplifting visions of a life with family by show's end. Nothing new should be expected in this formulaic exploitation of evanescent celebrity and this all too predictable corporate-style juggernaut.

In Webster's English dictionary, fame is defined as "the frenzy of renown." The frenzied, meaning people who are intoxicated by synthetic significance—are complicit in this farce. Forty years ago, in his book *The Image*, Daniel Boorstin argued that the graphic revolution in television had severed fame from greatness, which generally required a gestation period in which great deeds were performed. This severance hastened the decay of fame into mere notoriety, which is very plastic and very perishable.

The doctrine of "celebrity" triumphalism is inherently inclusive; it proceeds from the assumption that everyone already loves the wealthy and the pseudo-famous. Most pseudo-celebrities seems to have understood that their life is a constant conjuring trick. There is an incurable precariousness to their position as they try to live off derivative dignity from an anachronistic concept while cultivating the new royalism of a degraded democratic age—celebrity.

That assumption is what makes the "celebrity" circus so creepy. The pseudo-famous know that they owe their careers to the celebrity industry, know that their tabloid sensibility is well suited to a tabloid culture, know that the whole enterprise is built on bad faith. Still, the ratings continue to climb....

Will we start to emulate Julian Assange? Was that the original long-range agenda of the planners and schemers behind the WikiLeaks project? There are those who call Assange a Devil in disguise, with his white hair and a youthful, expressionless, baby face. In western tradition, Lucifer was a fallen angel, the most beautiful of God's creation. That is why the image is so powerful, much more than the written word, which requires some level of thought and conscious participation.

It is a question of perception. We often see the divine as 'sinister.' The other reflex is to see the demonic as divine. The image acts directly on the unconscious mind, conveying whole libraries of information in a single moment, setting up connecting links with other images, other ideas. That is why, frankly, the image is not to be trusted. One needs a powerful internal editor, one that questions each image to understand its purpose, its target, and its origins. We need another source of information. We need a context.

Meanwhile the original purpose of WikiLeaks is dead in the water. Thousands of mirror carcasses float on the Internet sea, none offering new material except the dribbles from the cables which at the current rate will require the passive sites to last redundantly decades when they could be offering valid material.

Lights. Camera. Action!

"The tomb opens, but instead of the ghoulish entities, only flowers emerge in the presence of the Truth.... [And we] saw that all we had been told was a story and that death does not exist."[80]

Madrid,
February 22, 2012

186

(ENDNOTES)

CHAPTER 3

1   Peter Levenda, *Sinister Forces, Book Two: A Warm Gun*, TrineDay, 2006, pp. 287-288.

2   Peter Levenda, *Sinister Forces, Book One: The Nine*, TrineDay, 2005, pp. 181.

3   http://Wikileaks.org/About.html

4   http://cryptome.org/Wikileaks/wikileaks-leak.htm

5   Neil Sheehan, Hendrick Smith, E.W. Kenworthy, Fox Butterfield, *The Secret History of the Vietnam War*, Unabridged Edition, NY Times, July 1971, pp. ix-x.

6   http://en.wikisource.org/wiki/United_States-Vietnam_Relations,_1945-1967:_A_Study_Prepared_by_the_Department_of_Defense

7   Neil Sheehan, *The Secret History of the Vietnam War, Pentagon Papers*, Bantam Books, p. x.

8   http://en.wikisource.org/wiki/United_States-Vietnam_Relations,_1945-1967:_A_Study_Prepared_by_the_Department_of_Defense

9   L. Marcus, "The Real CIA – The Rockefeller's Fascist Establishment," *The Campaigner*, April 1974, p.9. http://www.campaigner-unbound.0catch.com/real_cia_rockefellers_fascist_establishment.htm

10   L.Fetcher Prouty, *The Secret Team, the CIA and its allies in Control of the USA and the world*, 1973, http://www.ratical.org/ratville/JFK/ST/

11   Ibid.

12   L. Marcus, "The Real CIA – The Rockefeller's Fascist Establishment," *The Campaigner*, April 1974, p.9.

13   Ibid.

14   Ibid.

15   www.rand.org, History & Mission.

16   L. Marcus, "The Real CIA – The Rockefeller's Fascist Establishment," *The Campaigner*, April 1974, p.10.

17   Edward Spannaus, "When U.S. Joint Chiefs Planned Terror Attacks on America," *EIR*, October 12, 2001.

18   L. Marcus, "The Real CIA – The Rockefeller's Fascist Establishment," *The Campaigner*, April 1974.

19   F. William Engdahl, "WikiLeaks: A Big Dangerous US Government Con Job," globalresearch.ca, December 10, 2010.

20   Ronald West, "Julian Assange, Agent Provocateur," AlterNet blog, October, 11, 2010. http://blogs.alternet.org/penucquem/2010/10/11/julian-assange-cia-agent-provocateur/

21   L. Fletcher Prouty, *The Secret Team: The CIA and its Allies in control of the United States and the world*, 1973, Reprinted by Ballantine, 1991.

22   Ronald West, "Julian Assange, Agent Provocateur," AlterNet blog, October, 11, 2010.

23   F. William Engdahl, "WikiLeaks: A Big Dangerous US Government Con Job," December 7, 2010, http://www.engdahl.oilgeopolitics.net/Geopolitics___Eurasia/US_Con_Job/us_con_job.html.

24   "Afghanistan war logs: Story behind biggest leak in intelligence history," Nick Davies, *Guardian*, July 25, 2010.

25   Declan McCullagh, "Wikileak's estranged co-founder becomes critic (Q&A), July 20, 2010. http://news.cnet.com/8301-31921_3-20011106-281.html

26   Ibid.

27   *cryptome.org/0002/wl-diary-mirror.htm.*

28   "WikiLeaks: A Big Dangerous US Government Con Job," F. William Engdahl, December 10 2010, globalresearch.ca.

29   Ed Encho, "Main Core, Promis and the Shadow Government," http://existentialistcowboy.blogspot.com/2009/01/main-core-promis-and-shadow-government.html, January 26, 2009.

31   Scott Creighton, "If We Lose our Internet Freedoms Because of WikiLeaks, You Should At Least Know Why," December 11, 2010. http://globalresearch.ca/index.php?context=va&aid=22371. Quoting John Young, "Architect John Young: WikiLeaks Fog of Infowar and its Ties to The Elite - Alex Jones Tv 3/3," December 9, 2010. http://www.youtube.com/watch?v=d7ve_ez3LL0&feature=player_embedded#%21.

32   Steve Watson, Prisonplanet.com, "False Flag Cyber Attack could take down the Internet," Jul 21st, 2010.

33   Kurt Nimmo, "Pentagon's Cyber Command Prepares War Against the American People, infowars.com, May 23, 2010. http://www.infowars.com/pentagons-cyber-command-prepares-war-against-the-american-people/

34   Ibid.

35   Ibid.

36   Ibid.

37   "WikiLeaks and the Worldwide Information War Power, Propaganda, and the Global Political Awakening," Andrew Gavin Marshall, December 6, 2010, globalresearch.ca.

38   William F. Engdahl, "WikiLeaks: A Big Dangerous US Government Con Job," globalresearch.ca, December 10, 2010.

39   Kurt Nimmo, "Pentagon's Cyber Command Prepares War Against the American People," infowars.com, May 24, 2010

40   Ibid.

41   Alex Spillius, "Cyber attack 'could fell US within 15 minutes,'" Telegraph, January, 17, 2012, http://www.telegraph.co.uk/news/worldnews/northamerica/usa/7691500/Cyber-attack-could-fell-US-within-15-minutes.html

42   Kurt Nimmo, "Pentagon's Cyber Command Prepares War Against the American People," infowars.com, May 24, 2010.

43   Steve Watson, "False Flag Cyber Attack Could Takedown The Internet," PrisonPlanet, Jul 21,2010. http://www.prisonplanet.com/false-flag-cyber-attack-could-takedown-the-internet.html

44   Steve Aquino, "Should Obama Control the Internet?" *Mother Jones,* April 2, 2009. http://motherjones.com/politics/2009/04/should-obama-control-internet.

45   Steve Watson, "False Flag Cyber Attack Could Takedown The Internet," prisonplanet.com, July 21, 2010.

46   Siobhan Gorman, Details of "Einstein" Cyber Shield Disclosed by White House, *WSJ,* March 2, 2010.

47   Kurt Nimmo, "Pentagon's Cyber Command Prepares War Against the American People," infowars.com, May 24, 2010.

48   Steve Watson, "False Flag Cyber Attack Could Takedown The Internet," PrisonPlanet, Jul 21,2010.

49   Peter Beaumont, "US appoints first cyber warfare general," The Observer, May 22, 2010

50   http://www.eff.org/issues/nsa-spying

51   Steve Watson, "False Flag Cyber Attack Could Takedown The Internet," Prison-

Planet, Jul 21,2010.

52   Ibid.

53   Kurt Nimmo, "Pentagon's Cyber Command Prepares War Against the American People," infowars.com, May 24, 2010.

54   http://cryptome.org/0002/wl-diary-mirror.htm

55   http://cryptome.org/0002/wl-diary-mirror.htm

56   Ibid.

57   Ibid.

58   John Chuckman, "Bush at the UN," *Counterpunch*, September 25, 2003. http://www.counterpunch.org/2003/09/25/bush-at-the-un/

59   N. Ram, "Future Tibet," *Frontline*, Volume 24, Issue 14, July 14-27, 2007. http://www.flonnet.com/fl2414/stories/20070727005200400.htm

60   Calvin Coolidge, *Have Faith in Massachusetts*, Houghton Mifflin Company, 1919, p.69.

61   Daniel Estulin, "Breaking the Silence, Bilderberg Report, Part II," May 2005. www.nexusmagazine.com.

62   WikiLeaks on *BBC Culutre Show* with John Young, Cryptome.org, http://cryptome.org/0001/bbc-cryptome.htm, January 29, 2010.

63   http://en.wikipedia.org/wiki/Whistleblower

64   http://cryptome.org/0001/bbc-cryptome.htm, *BBC Culture Show*, January 28, 2010

65   Ibid.

66   Andrew Gavin Marshall, "WikiLeaks and the world-wide information war," globalresearch.ca, December 6, 2010.

67   Ibid.

68   *Russia Today* interview with John Young, January 2, 2011.

69   John Young, *BBC Culture Show*, January 28, Kieran Yeates, January 28, 2010.

70   Andrew Gavin Marshall, "WikiLeaks and the world-wide information war," globalresearch.ca, December 6, 2010.

71   Ibid.

72   Ibid.

73   Richard Stengel, Transcript: *TIME* Interview with WikiLeaks' Julian Assange, Time Magazine, December 1, 2010. http://www.time.com/time/printout/0,8816,2034040,00.html

74   Andrew Gavin Marshall, "WikiLeaks and the Worldwide Information War," globalresearch.ca, December 6, 2010.

75   Peter Levenda, *Sinister Forces: Vol. III; The Manson Secret*, TrineDay, 2006, p. 440.

76   F. William Engdahl, *Full Spectrum Dominance*, pp.278-279, 2008.

77   Peter Levenda, *Sinister Forces: Book III-The Mason Secret*, Trineday Press, 2006, p.440.

78   John Young, *BBC Culture Show*, January 28, Kieran Yeates, January 28, 2010.

79   Susan J. Drucker,Robert S. Cathcart, *American Heroes in a Media Age*, Hampton Press, 1994, pp. 19.

80   Peter Levenda, *Sinister Forces: Book I-The Nine*, Trineday Press, 2005, p.208.